The Shock of the Old

Philip Wilkinson

The Shock of the Old

A Guide to British Buildings

First published 2000 by Channel 4 Books

This edition published 2001 by Channel 4 Books, an imprint of Pan Macmillan Ltd,
Pan Macmillan, 20 New Wharf Road, London N1 9RR.
Basingstoke and Oxford.

Associated companies throughout the world.

www.panmacmillan.co.uk

ISBN 0 7522 6178 9

9 8 7 6 5 4 3 2 1

A CIP catalogue record for this book is available from the British Library.

Design by Jane Coney
Colour reproduction by Speedscan
Printed in the EC

This book accompanies the television series *The Shock of the Old*
made by Uden Associates for Channel 4.
Executive producer: Patrick Uden
Producer/Directors: Mark James and Jessica Whitehead

Introduction   6

Chapter One
romans@britannia.co.uk
The architecture of the invaders   12

Chapter Two
High and Mighty
The medieval cathedral builders   42

Chapter Three
The Smoke Filled Room
From hall-house to country house   72

Contents

Chapter Four
Built to Order
The classical style and the Georgian house 102

Chapter Five
The Manic Street Builders
The Victorian revolution in building   132

Chapter Six
The White Stuff
The many styles of modern architecture   164

Index   191

Introduction

We are used to the idea that new art and architecture can be provocative and disturbing. Nowadays, because all architects – and clients – want advance publicity for their buildings, the shocks often start long before the foundations are dug. Daniel Liebeskind's projected building for the Victoria and Albert Museum is a case in point: an alien, angular white spiral among the Victorian façades of South Kensington. Its shape was instantly controversial, dividing critics and starting arguments in the press. The arguments centred on the outside appearance of the building and not, with one or two honourable exceptions, on how well or badly it would work as part of a museum. It was the initial impact of the structure that concerned the objectors, the shock that it would create among its cosy South Kensington neighbours.

The V&A spiral is an extreme case, but throughout the country new buildings are causing controversy. Conservationists rage against encroachment on the countryside and the despoiling of city centres. Planners argue about the amount of housing that is needed and where it should be built. The press makes good copy out of buildings that fail to stand up to expectations, or fail to stand up at all.

The title of Robert Hughes's 1980 television series on modern art encapsulated this idea in a phrase: *The Shock of the New*. Hughes's series, and the landmark book that followed it, described many of the ways in which artists during the twentieth century shocked the public into new perceptions and fresh ways of seeing a variety of subjects, from propaganda to pleasure, utopia to the unconscious.

This new book and the television series it accompanies look at the story of building in Britain as a similar series of shock waves – buildings in new, unexpected styles, that are made of unusual or outlandish materials, that contrast with what went before, that use new technology in creative ways, that challenge our ideas of what a particular building type should be like, or that simply stand out from their surroundings. Throughout history, builders and architects have created surprises like these, revolutions in architecture that began at least as early as the Romans and that have justified the use of the phrase *The Shock of the Old*. To preserve some of the freshness of Piers Gough's commentory in the television series, some of his comments have been included in the book as marginal quotations.

CHANGING BUILDINGS

The shock waves created by architecture have been caused by many different types of structures. Buildings which we now take for granted – Norman cathedrals, Palladian mansions, Victorian railway stations – were outlandish in their time, as we can see by comparing them with what went before. They were also allowed to stand out in their neighbourhoods, something that today's architects have to fight for. Medieval cathedral builders did not have to worry if their towers and spires dwarfed the surrounding houses. Eighteenth-century nobles could sweep away entire villages to provide space and settings for their country houses.

The age of buildings like these makes them seem less shocking today. That is partly because we are used to them. They have established themselves as part of our culture and 'heritage'. It is also because, in many cases, the buildings themselves have changed. When we enter a medieval church or cathedral today the dominant colour is that of the stone, and many of the windows have clear glass. In the Middle Ages things were different. The walls were painted in bright colours; the windows glowed with stained glass. Even the statues were painted. The use of paint and gilding, and the coloured light thrown on to floors and walls by the sun shining through stained glass, made every visit to a cathedral a new surprise.

There are other ways in which buildings have changed and lost some of their original power to shock. Traditional half-timbered 'black and white' structures were not all black and white when they were first built. They could be red and white, or grey and yellow, and these colour schemes made them stand out from their surroundings even more than they do today. Another change is in the way interiors are lit. Electric light, even of the minimal kind now imposed in many old houses for conservation reasons, lacks the flickering, suspenseful drama created by candles, which made Georgian mouldings and carvings cast weird shadows, animating interiors in ways now rarely seen.

Even if a building remains basically the same, changes in its setting can affect how it relates to its surroundings. The great Elizabethan country houses, with their acres of windows symmetrically arranged, must have looked bizarre in their bright new stone. Centuries of weathering make them seem less brash, and they are softened further by the growth of trees around them, which seem to ease the buildings back into the landscape.

SHOCKS AND MEANINGS

A structure could shock because of what it stood for. The Romans were the first people to build and plan on a national scale in Britain. When they put up a fort or constructed Hadrian's Wall, their building projects embodied a message: 'We are your rulers. You will have to fight to throw us out.' The neat stonework and uniform planning only reinforced this, reminding Britons that here was an empire with unprecedented resources and vast manpower, backed by a host of craft skills that had hardly been dreamed of in Britain. Norman cathedrals must have had something of the same impact on a nation recently invaded from across the Channel.

But buildings, even big ones, do not always speak of oppression. The huge railway stations built by the Victorians sent a different message to their users. Travel across the country was suddenly faster and easier than ever before and goods were hauled at speed over hundreds of miles, opening up new markets for industry. The great arching train sheds of stations like Paddington and St Pancras were symbols of opportunity, and the size of that opportunity, like the size of the train sheds, was a surprise in itself.

In the early twentieth century modern architecture brought different sets of meanings. Gleaming white concrete houses, for example, fitted out with balconies and sun decks, seemed to encourage a lifestyle of sunbathing, exercise, and breakfast on the terrace in air as fresh and clean as their walls. The shock here was the suggestion that a building could change our way of life – a shock quickly tempered by the realization that such a change would not be a good idea in the British climate.

TECHNOLOGY AND CHANGE

Some of the greatest surprises in the story are the result of new technologies. These frequently involve the work of builders, for buildings are as much their creations as they are creations of architects – and architects have had little or no involvement in many British structures. Roman walls and roads were built by soldiers; half-timbered halls in the Middle Ages were created by carpenters; Georgian builders often followed printed pattern books without recourse to an architect; engineers were the prime movers in many Victorian structures, from train sheds to greenhouses.

This book pays tribute to the richness of vernacular architecture by looking at some of the key crafts involved in building at different periods – from mosaic-making to stone masonry, timber framing to the production of bricks. The variety of trades seems like a store of tradition today, as we look back nostalgically to the craft of the medieval quarryman, at one with the stone he was extracting, or marvel at the subtle hues still seen in handmade bricks. Traditional materials like these were often made locally and today seem to blend in with the landscape.

But building crafts could also make shock waves. Most people think of bricks as the most traditionally British of house-building materials. But in the seventeenth century they were colourful new ingredients, little used before. And architects carried on using them in surprising ways. The polychrome brick buildings of High Victorian architect William Butterfield, with their stripes and patterns, remain some of the most amazing structures in Britain; at the end of the twentieth century, Postmodern architects were again creating dazzling patterns with different-coloured bricks. The same goes for the renewed enthusiasm for mosaics, originally a Roman form of flooring, during the Victorian period. And the endlessly renewed fascination that glass has for architects and builders from medieval period and into the twenty-first century. In each case a traditional technology is renewed, revised, and reinvented, producing visual shocks and surprises along the way.

FASHION AND STYLE

Architectural styles and fashions change and develop in different ways. There are the sweeping, broad-brush movements that carry with them fundamental stylistic change – the adoption of the pointed-arched Gothic style in the thirteenth century, say, or the arrival of classicism in the seventeenth century. Within these broad movements are the smaller, subtler alterations in architectural fashion, such as the separate phases of medieval Gothic or the different versions of the classical style – inspired variously by Greek, Roman, or Renaissance originals – that were developed during the eighteenth century. A short book like this cannot chart every trend in design fashion. But it can give an idea of the sorts of changes that took place, of the variety of British buildings, and of the way in which playing variations on a style could produce another kind of shock to Britain's visual system.

It can also suggest that styles and buildings are not always clear-cut. Every structure develops over time. It can be extended, rebuilt, or refurbished. As a result, a large old building often displays elements from several different styles. Britain's cathedrals are the most notable examples of this. Gloucester – which began life as an abbey church in the seventh century – is famous as an example of the Norman architecture of the eleventh century. But it was also remodelled in the fourteenth century and its choir, Lady chapel, tower, and cloisters are some of the earliest and finest examples of the English Perpendicular style.

In the nineteenth century the Gothic style was revived, and was a favourite of church architects for the entire Victorian period. There's nothing shocking in that, of course. The Victorians were drawing on a long tradition of Gothic church building. But they also extended and elaborated the style, producing structures quite unlike their medieval predecessors. Making new shapes, importing brilliant foreign materials such as marble, and incorporating new technology, Victorian architects made Gothic new. Their town halls and hotels can still amaze us today.

COUNTRY AND CITY

This book draws its examples from both urban and rural environments. It finds the city, endlessly renewing and regenerating itself from the Roman period to the present, a dynamo of architectural innovation, constantly interesting and continuously changing. But the countryside also has its moments of shock. Nothing can take the breath away like the first view of a Palladian mansion, glimpsed in the distance as one rounds the curve of a drive through a park. Few interior spaces are as awesome as the great medieval barns with their elegantly engineered timber roofs.

Everywhere we go, we can find buildings that have this dramatic effect, either revealing their qualities slowly in a series of spaces like an ancient cathedral, or creating an instantaneous impact like a medieval hall. Many modern architects are interested in the ways in which their predecessors in earlier periods designed their buildings and rose to the challenges of construction, decoration, and the organization of space. Each of the historical chapters therefore includes a feature on the way certain recent architecture reflects the buildings of the past. These show, for example, how modern architects have used new technology to create generous, overarching spaces that recall medieval cathedrals, or how a modern housing development can take something from the order and elegance of a Georgian terrace. Links like these, back into architectural history and forward to the present, form a rich and challenging tradition, one on which architects continue to draw in the twenty-first century.

chapter one

romans@ britannia.co.uk

THE ARCHITECTURE OF THE INVADERS

▸ Piers Gough near the reconstructed Roman wall at Wallsend.

Rome's impact on Britain was enormous, and we still feel its effects today. We travel along roads first surveyed by its engineers and many towns were founded by the Romans. Their style of building is still a powerful influence on some architects. Citizens of a great power whose empire stretched across Europe to western Asia and northern Africa, the Romans must have seemed awesome to the native people of Britain in the first century AD. Their whole approach to conquest and government – their planning, their military discipline, the arrow-straight precision of their roads – would have been alien. And the Romans built – forts, temples, basilicas, city walls, gatehouses – on a scale unknown to Britons. The period when they occupied Britain seems a natural place to begin this survey of building.

BUILDERS OF THE IRON AGE

Iron Age houses that have been reconstructed at Butser Ancient Farm in Hampshire show that the Britons were already skilled builders when the Romans arrived. The largest is some 15 metres in diameter and is dominated by a conical thatched roof above quite low walls of wattle and daub. Apart from a protruding entrance porch it is completely round. Inside, the structure is clearly visible. As well as the outer wall there is an inner ring of wooden posts joined to the roof timbers, the largest of which are six principal rafters that soar up to the apex. Because of their length, these tend to bow under their own weight so, near the top, an ingenious hexagonal arrangement of six wooden

▲ Reconstructed Iron Age house at Butser Ancient Farm.

braces holds them apart and keeps them from bowing, maintaining the 45-degree slope needed to throw off the rain.

This type of house is an impressive structure. Its builders could handle timber with confidence and although they felled some 220 trees to make it, the circular form is economical, enclosing a large volume that uses fewer materials than an equivalent rectangular building. Its round shape also reduces wind resistance, an important design feature in seaboard locations, such as Brittany and north-western Spain, where houses like this were also built.

The house was heated by a central fire but there was no chimney or smoke hole, an arrangement that looks primitive to modern eyes. However, it conceals good sense and working knowledge: smoke from the fire filtered safely through the thatch while a smoke hole might have drawn sparks towards the roof.

Iron Age building was therefore far from primitive, a point Dr Peter Reynolds, director of Butser Ancient Farm, is eager to make: 'Most people, when they talk about prehistory, talk about huts. This makes me very angry because everybody thinks of a hut as something ... built by people who are poor, struggling individuals, hoping to reach civilization, which is the gift of the Romans. What absolute nonsense! ... This building is probably more complex structurally than a Roman temple.' Well adapted to local needs and conditions as these houses were, the Romans had other ideas.

'LIKE A TIMBER STONEHENGE'

THE ROMAN CONQUEST

In AD 43 the Romans arrived in Britain in force. They brought four legions and a large number of auxiliary troops, perhaps as many as 50,000 well-disciplined men in total. Their leaders included Vespasian and Galba, who would later become emperors: this was a high-profile, important expedition.

Having landed, probably at Richborough in Kent, they advanced north-west, inflicting heavy blows on the Britons near the Thames before moving on to the British capital at Colchester (Camulodunum). The town was soon captured and no doubt many native leaders began to make peace with the invaders. One who had put up a fight, Caractacus, retreated to Wales from where he was to mount guerrilla attacks on the Romans. But large areas of the country were subdued by the time the emperor Claudius made his triumphal entry into Rome in AD 44, the year after his successful invasion of Britain.

The Romans set up bases for stores at strategic points on the coast such as Richborough in Kent and Fishbourne in West Sussex. The fleet could moor near depots like these so that extra stores could be brought in or troops moved rapidly around the coast. The army also pushed inland across Britain. As they did so, they set up forts as bases and centres of local government, many of which grew into towns connected by the roads the Romans built across the British countryside.

They did not take over the whole of Britain at one go. The east of England fell quite rapidly (in spite of an Iceni revolt in AD 47), but it took a series of military campaigns for them to gain control over more far-flung areas such as the west, the Welsh borders, and the far north. Even so, the legions moved fast to Romanize Britain, laying down the administrative structure that controlled their new province.

The Romans transformed Britain. The legionaries included in their ranks skilled builders and representatives of every trade from glass-maker to iron-worker, as well as surveyors who laid out building sites and oversaw construction. The auxiliaries provided labour, and the discipline was such that major building projects could be

▼ Stane Street, West Sussex, a preserved section of Roman road.

accomplished with speed. To begin with, they mainly used local timber so fortresses and other structures could be erected very quickly.

Although many of the buildings were unremarkable to look at, Britons would have been impressed by the way they were organized. Fortresses, the first structures to be built, were made to a set pattern which could be varied to take account of local conditions and requirements. Roads paid no respect to local features – they carved a straight path across the country, cutting through fields and crossing rivers as required. And they were all built in a similar, military way, with firm foundations, tough stone facings, and drains to take care of water. They were the first decent roads in Britain and the Romans' singularity of purpose in building them must have been impressive.

'THE M1 OF ITS DAY'

Roman roads

Most roads in Rome's conquered provinces were built by the army and were first and foremost a means of getting from one military stronghold to another, and of marching troops around newly occupied territory. Although other early civilizations had built roads, no culture had produced so many straight ones in such a variety of different terrains. The ranks of the Roman army clearly included accomplished surveyors who could establish and keep a straight course. This famed straightness was an expression of Roman might – never before had a single power been able to dominate the entire island of Britain in this way. The distances involved, and the singleness of purpose, must have been overwhelming to the local people.

Once the Roman engineers had established their straight line and cleared the ground of trees, rocks, and other obstructions, they dug a trench which could be a metre or more deep. Into it they put a solid foundation of large stones, laid so that they provided support and allowed water to drain away. This base layer was followed by a thick layer of sand or gravel, sometimes mixed with clay. Finally this was topped with a paving layer of flat stones, which gave a surface that was not as smooth as that on a modern road, but just as hard. The surface could be cambered like roads are today and edged with kerbstones. Ditches on either side of the carriageway were dug to carry away surface water.

Roads made as well as this had not been seen in Britain before – and would not be seen again until the advances in road-building that were made during the eighteenth and nineteenth centuries by engineers such as Thomas Telford. They were so good that they were used for centuries, and many form the basis for modern routes today. The fact that a number of Roman forts became major towns has meant that these routes are as strategic today as they were to the Romans 2,000 years ago.

RICHBOROUGH

When they really wanted to impress, the Romans built in a truly monumental way. Richborough, Kent, an early stores depot, seems to have been built as the gateway to the province of Britain. Its buildings included a fortress here, but more magnificent still was its triumphal arch: tall, with foundations some 10 metres deep and a structure that towered 25 metres above ground level, it was clad in specially imported white marble that radiated light and was visible miles out to sea. The marble was unlike any building material in Britain and the arch, crowned with classical statuary, was a typically Roman form that was foreign to native builders.

The Richborough arch was erected in honour of Claudius and was an advertisement for the conquerors' success. The legions could march triumphantly through it and on to Watling Street, the great Roman road that led to London and then across the country to Chester. To Britons, the entire spectacle

◀ Reconstruction of the triumphal arch, Richborough.

'BRITAIN'S FIRST SHOPPING MALL'

must have seemed both awe-inspiring and alien. Other innovations included a *mansio* (a complex with accommodation for high-ranking soldiers) a bathhouse, and leisure facilities. Among the most notable introductions were shops arranged like an early form of shopping centre.

All that is left of Claudius's great arch are its symmetrical concrete foundations, and the remains that are now visible date from the third century when the Roman Empire was beginning to break up and Saxons, from what is now Germany, threatened the shore of Britain. The authorities saw the need for stronger defences and the Romans erected massive walls around the fortress, demolishing the arch in the process and using much of the stone for the new fortifications. Ditches were built around the walls to create an area in which attackers could be isolated, allowing the soldiers inside the fort to concentrate their fire.

Imposing stone walls still mark the boundaries of the fortress and are thick, still quite tall, and made of a facing of ashlar blocks with an infill of flint and mortar. The quality of the masonry and the block sizes are variable, suggesting that the walls were built at speed – possibly because of the threatened invasion – by several different gangs of workers: the joins where one gang met another and the stone does not match are still visible.

Throughout Britain the Romans built forts which, though they would not have had great walls like Richborough, were nevertheless impressive. The plan was usually a playing-card shape – a rectangle with rounded corners – with the barrack blocks and stables laid out in neat rows within it and a headquarters building at the centre. This regularity of pattern, and the grid-like arrangement of the buildings, was another alien feature in Britain. It was a feature that was reproduced when the Romans expanded some forts into fully fledged towns.

TOWNS

Roman towns developed for a number of reasons. Legionaries discharged from the army needed somewhere to live and various new towns were founded in Britain as a result, often adjacent to forts. Others developed when the Romans built forts next to existing British settlements which then expanded into towns. In addition, towns developed near forts because a large military presence attracted traders and markets. The invaders encouraged native leaders to Romanize – to educate their children in the Roman fashion and to adopt a Roman lifestyle – and Romanized Britons were often eager to emulate the city life of their rulers, leading to more urban developments. As a result, dozens of towns were founded, or smaller settlements expanded into towns, in the Roman period. However, it did not happen quickly and it was sometimes decades before a town had its full complement of houses, streets, public buildings, and defences. Often, especially to begin with, the buildings were made of wood rather than the stone or brick structures for which the Romans are famous today. But they were still very different from what had gone before.

The difference started at the most basic level, with the town plan: streets were straight and arranged in a grid pattern, a plan that is easy to organize and lay out, convenient for deliveries, simple for everyone. The Romans understood its benefits and the city block, or *insula*, was as familiar to them as it is to a modern New Yorker. Specialist aerial photographs show street grids still visible on some sites but most Roman cities have been submerged under later buildings, with only hints left in the modern road layout.

▾Floors and foundations of Roman buildings near Hadrian's wall.

The new architecture that was built on this grid plan used mortared stonework with dressed stone blocks, clay tiles for the roofs, and columns, vaults, and arches. As far as we can tell most of these features were new to Britain as local workers would not have known how to build them. The

'THE GRID IS THE PLANNING OF THE CONQUEROR'

Romans had to bring in their own craftworkers, some of whom may have come from Italy, others from nearby provinces such as Gaul. British builders were soon copying their techniques, as the Gauls and other conquered peoples had done before them.

At the heart of a Roman town was the forum, a public space around which were a number of buildings that provided the focus for administration, commerce, justice, and religious life. Along one side of the forum was the basilica. This large public building acted as the headquarters of local government and courts were also held there. Basilicas were usually long and hall-like, often with a nave and side aisles, a plan that was later imitated in Christian churches. The forum also contained temples and, although these were not usually the imposing structures they were in Europe, they were still impressive buildings. Nearby there might also be an amphitheatre for entertainments, and the public bath complex.

The forum buzzed with activity. The townspeople came to it to socialize and do business and stalls were set up there on market days. In the background were buildings in the Roman style which, as well as offering all the convenience of city life, also reminded the inhabitants of the greater community of the empire and the overarching power of the emperor.

VERULAMIUM

Many Roman towns, from Lincoln to Gloucester, Exeter to York, were so successful that they lasted for centuries and were overbuilt in later architectural styles. The remains of Roman buildings are minimal in such places. A few sites, however, like Wroxeter, Shropshire, and Verulamium (St Albans) in Hertfordshire were not much overbuilt and the typical Roman layout can still be seen.

Verulamium was originally built soon after the conquest near the capital of a local Belgic tribe, one of the important centres of ancient British life. It was destroyed during Boudicca's revolt in AD 69 and rebuilt during the following twenty years. The Roman grid plan is clearly discernible, interrupted only by the line of the ancient Watling Street, which enters the town at a diagonal from the south. Although much of the forum is now beneath a later church, Verulamium's temples and theatre have been excavated. The latter is an example of how structures in the provinces differed from those in Rome. A Roman citizen would have expected to see two separate types of building for entertainment: a theatre with a stage and an amphitheatre with a central arena surrounded by banks of seats. The theatre at Verulamium is a combination of these two forms, a design that came to Britain from Gaul.

The foundations of shops and houses that have been excavated at St Albans show that many houses were originally built of timber before being rebuilt in stone during the second century – a development that would have made the town look even more alien to the local population. Similarly, the interiors – at least in the houses of the richer inhabitants – would have looked very different. Finds preserved in the museum at St Albans include fragments from the painted plasterwork in the interiors of some of the higher-status houses. In Italy, rich Romans lined rooms with marble, which was both cool and elegant. Although Britain has no marble and there is little need to keep cool, Romanized Britons liked the idea of elegant, coloured interiors. The occasional, very rich, individual like the person who lived in the vast Roman palace at Fishbourne, West Sussex, was able to import marble, but otherwise walls were painted to imitate features such as mouldings, cornices, and panelling that might have been made of marble in Rome. As the fragments at St Albans show, because the fresco technique – painting the plaster while it is still wet so that the colour penetrates below the surface – was used for this, some of the colour has survived. It is bright (though less bright than it would have been originally), and some painters worked with more care than others. But the fragments show that the Romans valued colour. As Professor T.F.C. Blagg, senior lecturer in archaeology at the University of Kent, put it: 'One of the things which can take people by surprise is how colourful the ancient world was. There was a view, which mainly comes from galleries of marble sculpture, which makes the classical world look rather cold and white ... But people forget that ancient sculpture was actually painted ... It was a very colourful world altogether.'

▸ St Albans cathedral tower, showing reused Roman bricks.

In about AD 200 a wall of masonry was built to defend Verulamium, a task that would have required additional resources and labour and included transporting tens of thousands of cartloads of building materials. This move towards a more solid, long-lasting, masonry-built town was probably reproduced in many settlements in Roman Britain as more resources became available and the local population became more Romanized.

Materials, such as bricks and clay tiles, that the Romans introduced transformed the townscapes in many settlements – and are virtually identical to those used today. Bricks, after all, are still thought of as the quintessential British building material. Pantiles are still widespread in many parts of the Mediterranean. Terrazzo floors, made by grinding down the surface of Roman concrete, are common in public buildings all over the world. Although these are durable materials remarkably few of them remain in situ. However, they were often re-used after the Romans left. The medieval cathedral at St Albans (ironically built in honour of a Christian martyr who was killed by the Romans) is made largely of recycled Roman bricks. It is the only large complete building standing in Britain that is made mainly of Roman materials.

The threat to security as the Roman Empire began to break up meant that defences had to be strengthened, and thick walls and solid gatehouses joined the other Roman monuments in British towns. Meanwhile, in the countryside, a similar move towards grander, more permanent structures was also taking place.

BIGNOR ROMAN VILLA

Some of the most fascinating remains of Roman Britain are found in villas, country houses built by the more prosperous members of the population. These ranged from the equivalent of a small farmhouse to something as large as a palace, and most were probably occupied by native Britons who had won wealth and status. Just how much status can be seen by the size of some of the villas, their many rooms arranged around large courtyards, by the remains of elegant mosaic flooring, and by elaborate, multi-room bathhouses complete with underfloor heating.

A good example of a sizeable Roman villa was discovered in 1813 at Bignor, West Sussex. It began life at the end of the second century as a wooden structure with a simple rectangular block of rooms and later it was rebuilt in stone, tile, and concrete. The original range of rooms was extended so that the house surrounded three sides of a courtyard; a further area in front acted as a farmyard. Finally, in the fourth century, the courtyard was closed off with a fourth range, and the farmyard in front was surrounded by a wall.

At this stage Bignor had several features that marked it out as a house belonging to a high-status family. It was large and the outbuildings were also of a good size – the barn was big enough to accommodate as many as twelve teams of oxen for ploughing. The villa had a fountain and there was

▸ Reconstruction of
Bignor Roman Villa.

▸ Reconstruction of
the corridor mosaic
at Bignor.

a bath complex with quite large baths that were probably vaulted. Hollow bricks that would have made an arch shape have been discovered, suggesting that hot air and gases from the heating system passed up through the vault, warming the room.

Another grand feature is the dining room. Rectangular but with a semicircular apse at one end, it was the kind of room in which the Romans in Italy reclined on couches to dine. The couches were arranged in a group of three, hence the room's Latin name: *triclinium*. Rooms of this shape generally appear in the grander houses of Roman Britain, the homes of Britons who were highly Romanized. A visitor from a major city in Europe would have felt at home eating a meal here.

Bignor was built to impress and this is reflected in its mosaic floors. Even the entrance corridor had one and its walls would have been decorated with coloured paintwork – anyone who crossed the threshold would have been aware that they were entering the house of an important person. The surviving

Mosaics

Rich Romans decorated the floors of their houses with mosaics, patterns built up from thousands of tiny stones – tesserae – set in mortar. The skill of the craftsmen who made these lay in creating an effective design, keeping the surface flat, and placing the tesserae closely and evenly together. Mosaics were already fashionable in Italy and Gaul when the Romans arrived in Britain took place and the invaders brought accomplished mosaic-makers with them. By the second century AD British craftsmen had learned their techniques and a distinctly British mosaic style was developing. It was a style created by artisans, who usually followed patterns that were given to them.

These mosaic workers probably spent the frosty winter months gathering materials and making tesserae: red ones from pieces of broken pottery or tile, white from limestone or hard chalk, blue from shale or lias limestone, and yellow from natural stone. In addition, they occasionally made use of fragments of imported marble or pieces of glass. The mosaicist probably used a small anvil to chop the pottery and stone into pieces, which vary in size from 12.5 millimetres to a mere 5 millimetres across.

There were several different ways of laying the tesserae, some of which involved prefabricating the design on a sheet of linen before transferring it to the floor. For simpler mosaics, the craftsman worked directly on the floor. The process began with laying a rubble foundation covered with lime mortar. For a complex layout, the mosaic-maker often sketched the design first, either by scratching it into the damp mortar or painting it on to the surface, then laid the tesserae on the mortar so that the guide disappeared. Mosaicists worked from the centre outwards and if working 'freehand', without marking the design on the mortar, used tools like T-squares and compasses to ensure that the pattern kept to its intended shape and position. In better quality work, they could achieve great precision.

As each section was completed a thin mix of mortar was worked into the gaps between the tesserae, as grouting. An experienced craftsmen working on a simple mosaic with a standard pattern could probably lay at least a square metre of tesserae in a day; more complex designs would have taken rather longer.

corridor mosaic – some 24 metres of patterned tesserae – gives a hint of this importance, but originally it was about twice as long, with thousands of tesserae giving an impression of rich colour.

In other rooms, the subject matter of the mosaics shows how the owners aspired to the culture of Rome. The goddess Venus and gladiators from the

▲ Mosaic floor, Bignor
Roman Villa.

arena both reflect typically Roman pleasures. The images are beautifully put together with flashes of artistic achievement that the Romans would have appreciated. But much of the mosaic work, such as the standard patterns and borders, would have been produced by artisans who followed a template or reproduced a design that they had re-created dozens of times before.

Smaller villas or town houses would have had only simple mosaics, not even as high in quality as the borders at Bignor. Mosaic artists often made mistakes or cut corners. If they ran out of tesserae of the right colour, for example, they frequently changed to others, irrespective of the requirements of the design. Another common error was to get the intricate geometry of mosaic patterns wrong. Mosaicists could also misinterpret designs, especially ones that involved alien mythical beasts. One subject was the chimera, a creature with a cat-like head, serpent's tail, and a second head, that of a goat, on its back. British mosaic-makers, unfamiliar with classical mythology, were quite capable of making the second head more like that of a duck than a goat. Nevertheless, at their biggest and best the villas were as sophisticated as the buildings the Romans erected in their cities.

BATH

Aquae Sulis, modern Bath, was one of the most remarkable of the Romano-British cities. It developed in the mid to late first century around a hot spring (from which water still bubbles at 46.5°C) which was seen as a magical place with healing qualities. The Britons had founded a temple here to their goddess Sulis, one of the most important ancient British water deities, and Bath has been an important centre ever since. This is frustrating for anyone trying to study the Roman remains because the many layers of history – medieval, Georgian, and Victorian – that stand between the Roman period and today have to be mentally stripped away. Since the 1880s, however, when Aquae Sulis was first excavated, archaeologists have assembled a clear picture of the Roman city.

When the Romans arrived they identified Sulis with Minerva, goddess of war, patron of craftworkers, and healer. A town grew up around the spring and at its heart was her temple and the famous baths. So the city was first and foremost a religious place, where the extraordinary flow of water inspired awe, as Barry Cunliffe, professor of European archaeology at Oxford University, explains: 'It was essentially a great sacred place which both the Romans and the natives would have focused on. Water bubbles out of the ground at the rate of a

▲ The Roman Great Bath at Bath, surrounded by eighteenth-century buildings.

▲ Reconstruction of the interior of the Great Bath.

quarter of a million gallons a day, and it doesn't stop. It was a place of enormous mystery, where you could communicate with the gods.'

The temple of Sulis Minerva was an unusual building for Roman Britain. Unlike other Romano-British temples, it was in the classical style, with a portico held up by Corinthian columns and surmounted by a triangular pediment. On the pediment was a large carved stone roundel depicting a mythical creature, half gorgon and half native water god. Inside the temple was a bronze statue of Minerva, the head of which survives. The sophisticated, very Roman, style of the building would have marked Bath out as a special place.

So would the nearby great baths which were used in conjunction with the temple. After worshipping the goddess a visitor would throw an offering into the spring and then go to the bath complex for a relaxing, curative swim or soak.

Constructing the baths, with their exceptional water source, required exceptional engineering. The Romans controlled the flow from the spring as it had never been controlled before, siphoning clean water off the top of the incoming stream to supply the baths. When sediment built up in the spring they opened a sluice gate and as the water pushed through this it forced out the sediment, which passed away through a drain.

The main room in the bath compex was the hall, some 20 x 30 metres in size. It contained the great bath – much larger than any other in Britain – which was used for swimming and soaking in the curative water. Nearby, there were lead pipes along which hot water passed to a fountain and another, smaller, immersion pool. The pipes are still in position at the side of the bath. As well as the pools there were also steam rooms in which the air was heated artificially, as in a modern sauna.

Where necessary the builders used a form of concrete mixed with crushed tiles to make the structure waterproof. The great bath was also lined with lead – not only to keep the water in, but also to stop ground water seeping into the bath and polluting it. This thick lead lining still remains, holding the water as it did some 2,000 years ago.

The baths originally had a timber-framed roof that rested on pillars ranged along the sides of the pool, but after some sixty years it was replaced with a huge barrel vault like the ones that topped large public buildings in the major cities of the empire. The reason for this is not known. It may be that the roof timbers were warping in the heat; or perhaps the Romans simply wanted to make the building still grander.

Fragments of the vault can still be seen. It is an arching structure, and much of the facing is made of hollow, box-shaped clay tiles. Bonded together with concrete, the tiles provided a combination of strength and lightness that ensured the roof did not collapse under its own weight. The style is rather brutal, not unlike some twentieth-century concrete buildings, and probably shocked the early users of the baths in the same way that people in the twentieth century have been shocked by modern constructions in concrete.

The baths must have been spectacular, and some of that spectacle is re-created today by the largely nineteenth-century buildings that surround the great bath. But enough of the Roman work remains to show that Aquae Sulis was an exceptional Roman settlement and not typical of the time. The bath complex was large for a provincial building and, in dating from the first century, very early for a big masonry building in Roman Britain. Given these exceptional features, it is not surprising that craftworkers from Europe, including at least one sculptor from Gaul, worked on the complex. Aquae Sulis was magnificent, and very Roman, but we have to look elsewhere for buildings that are typical of Roman Britain.

HADRIAN'S WALL

Hadrian's Wall was the largest Roman building project in the province, and is still the most extensive set of Roman remains in Britain. The great fortification, which runs through northern England from Carlisle to Wallsend near the mouth of

'THE LEGIONS WERE LIKE OUR ROYAL ENGINEERS'

the River Tyne, was commissioned by the emperor Hadrian and built between AD 122 and 128 to counter border disturbances, control border crossings, and police the empire's northernmost frontier.

Originally the eastern part of the wall was built from stone and turf was used for the section to the west of the River Irthing, but after about forty years the turf was replaced with stone. The resulting wall stretched for 117 kilometres and was about 2 metres wide. We can only guess at the height: the tallest surviving portion stands at 3.1 metres so the original wall was perhaps 3.5 metres to 4 metres high. Every Roman mile (about 1.5 kilometres) along its length there was a small fort, now known as a milecastle, which provided accommodation for auxiliary troops who patrolled the wall. At regular intervals between each pair of milecastles were two guard turrets. More men were garrisoned in a further sixteen forts along the wall.

There were earthworks on either side of the wall: a V-shaped ditch to the north and, to the south, a flat-bottomed ditch, now usually called the vallum, which ran parallel to the wall some 35 metres away. The vallum winds its way around the wall forts, defining a 'military zone' south of the wall where troops could move freely and where much of the business of policing the border crossing took place.

◀ Hadrian's Wall, showing the core of rubble and concrete.

▲ A section of Hadrian's Wall.

For the Pictish people to the north, the wall and the soldiers who manned it were a constant reminder of the might of Rome. It was not an impregnable barrier – there were regular crossing points – but any enemy who wanted to challenge the empire by crossing in force was left in no doubt of the military power that could be unleashed from the wall's turrets, milecastles, and forts. Nevertheless, there were incursions from the north, notably in AD 196 and 296 when the wall was damaged and had to be repaired. In AD 367 and 369 the garrison saw action again. By this time the empire was weaker and the opposition stronger (Scots and Saxons had joined the Picts) and the Romans left the wall to the locals to concentrate on defending territories further south.

Hadrian's Wall was therefore a viable defensive system for some 240 years and during this time the soldiers who built it and manned it left a lasting impression on the countryside. Such a major project involved a formidable work force, as Alan Whitworth, Hadrian's Wall recording officer, explains: 'Three Roman legions were involved in the construction of the wall, eighteen thousand to twenty thousand men. The legions were not only major battle groups with front-line soldiers; they also included skilled carpenters, glaziers, iron-workers. They could build anything.'

Their work still looks impressive. Each surface of the wall is made up of squared masonry of blocks of local stone, taken from the many quarries nearby. The surfaces conceal an inner core of rubble and a 'concrete' made up of clay, sand, lime and water. The wall may have been covered with a protective coat of limewash or lime mortar. In other words, Hadrian's Wall was very much a standard Roman wall, on a large scale. It would not have been difficult to build, but getting materials to the site, in a cold hilly environment with the constant threat of harassment from the north, and organizing thousands of workers, was a challenge.

This challenge may be behind a rather odd feature of the wall. In many places thick foundations lead to narrower upper courses, indicating that the wall was originally intended to be wider than it was actually built. Perhaps the builders changed their minds because they were trying to cut down on stone, and thus also on the work of transporting it. Or perhaps the governor in charge wanted to finish the project quickly, during his term of office, and so take the full credit for it.

Glass

Iron Age round houses, like the ones reconstructed at Butser, had no windows and the only light came from the flames of the central fire, or through the door if it was left open in summer. 'Wind holes' were sometimes fitted but, like the door, they were covered with skins in all but the best weather. Using glass windows to let light into buildings was a Roman innovation and even small ones could transform a building's interior.

Glass had been made in Egypt and western Asia for thousands of years but in about 50 BC the Romans invented glass-blowing, a process that involves blowing an air bubble into a piece of hot, molten glass on the end of a blowpipe. As glass-workers developed their skill they were able to make vessels of many different shapes using this method, but it took them a while to work out how to make flat sheets of window glass.

The answer came late in the first century AD with the development of cylinder glass. The glass-worker shaped molten glass from the furnace on the end of a blowpipe and, by a combination of reheating, spinning, and blowing, made a cylinder of glass. Next, only the end of the cylinder was reheated and the glass-worker then burst this by blowing gently through the pipe. The cylinder was left to cool down and then it was split all the way along its length with a red-hot iron before being carefully reheated and opened out until a flat pane of glass was produced. After a session of heating in a kiln, the pane was allowed to cool down again so that it became tough and ready for use.

The process required the glass-worker to judge the temperature accurately. Too cold, and nothing would happen; too hot and the cylinder walls would stick to each other, or to the furnace. And the results were hardly spectacular by the standardsof modern glassmaking: small panes that were not even fully transparent. Traces of iron oxide in the glass gave it a green colour.

Glass-makers soon realized that raw materials — soda, lime, and sand — from different sources produced colour variations. Although these are often attractive in the vases and bowls displayed in museums, colour and iridescence pose a problem in window glass. So the Romans experimented until they had established which sources produced materials — mainly sands — that were the purest and most suitable for windows. They also discovered that adding certain chemicals, such as manganese dioxide, counterbalanced the iron oxide and produced a much clearer glass. Glass-making industries developed in areas with good sources of sand, notably in the eastern Mediterranean and around Cologne and Trier in Germany.

GATES, FORTS, AND BATHS

Reconstructions of fortifications on Hadrian's Wall give an idea of its scale and of the everyday lives of the Romans and the working buildings they constructed. At South Shields (Roman Arbeia), at the eastern end of the wall, archaeologists' reconstructions of the west gate of the fort and some of its walls demonstrate how

▲ The reconstructed Roman gateway at South Shields (Roman Arbeia).

▼ Remains of a hypocaust, showing the pillars that supported the floor.

challenging they would have looked to potential raiders. The details, especially the battlements and other upper parts, are educated guesswork but the reconstructions bring the ruins to life.

So do the remains of the places where the soldiers lived. The wall spawned many communities. In addition to the forts themselves, which were built to the usual 'playing-card' shape that enclosed rows of barracks, secondary, civilian settlements grew up next to many of them. Soldiers who had served their time in the army could settle in one of these – known as a vicus. They often married and raised families, many of whom became the next generation of soldiers manning the wall.

The bathhouse at Sedgedunum near Wallsend, Tyne and Wear, was constructed for the men in the garrison, but every Roman town had similar complexes. From the outside the one at Sedgedunum is rugged-looking with well-buttressed walls, a pantiled roof, and small windows. But the key to how the baths worked is inside, in the heating system. Brick pillars held up the floor, creating a void, and hot gases from a furnace passed between the pillars, heating the floor and the room above. Graham Tench, architect and expert in Roman reconstruction, explains how hot the room could become: 'When the fire is up to full temperature, this floor will be too hot to stand

Roman concrete

Concrete was probably first used as early as the fourth century BC, and examples in Rome survive from the third century. It was made by mixing a bonding agent, lime, with an aggregate such as sand, and then with water to make a plastic substance that would set hard. The aggregate was important because without it the lime would crack as it dried, shrinking and coming away from the masonry. The best aggregate was a volcanic sand, pozzolana, from north of the bay of Naples and around the base of Vesuvius. Concrete made with this would even set hard under water, making it invaluable in bridge-building. The next best aggregrate was made of river sand and broken tile fragments.

The most widespread use of concrete was in building walls with a rubble core. A pair of parallel facing walls of brick or stone were built in the normal way, but with a gap between them, and when a builder had completed several courses of masonry he filled this with concrete and rubble. Once set, the core was so strong that many ancient ones still stand, long after the facing material – often neatly trimmed blocks of stone – has been removed and re-used. This type of construction was ideal for the Romans. It could be achieved with small stones or bricks, which were easy to transport, and strong walls could be built at great speed, an important advantage for empire-builders in a hurry. Finally, it required less skilled labour than was needed for a wall made entirely of dressed stone blocks.

Concrete was also immensely useful for making vaults. Again there was the advantage of speed, together with the material's enormous strength when it is used to build the tunnel-like barrel vaults favoured by the Romans. The first step was to erect a wooden structure to support the wet concrete. This timber shuttering had to be curved correctly so that the finished vault was the right shape, and strong enough to take the enormous weight of the concrete. The Romans developed a way of building vaults that were supported during construction with a combination of timber scaffolding and tiles. The framework of the scaffolding held up the tiles and the concrete that formed the vault was poured on top. Once the concrete was set, the wood was removed and the tiles remained on the ceiling.

Concrete gave the Romans a tremendous structural advantage. It enabled them to complete engineering projects, including bridges and aqueducts, that would have been very difficult without it. But concrete provided another benefit: a 'plastic' material, it enables different-shaped spaces to be created with ease. Largely as a result of concrete, Roman architects could develop a range of different room shapes – octagons, circles, semicircular apses, as well as domes and semidomes – which had previously been rare or unknown. Baths, basilicas, even the dining rooms of large villas, benefited. The new material changed the vocabulary of architectural space.

on with your bare feet.' The Romans overcame this problem by wearing wooden clogs to protect their feet. The hot gases could also travel up through channels or tubular tiles on the walls to bring extra heat into the

'THE WORLD'S FIRST CENTRAL HEATING SYSTEM'

room. This ingenious system allowed several of the bathhouse's high interior rooms to be heated to different temperatures.

A bathhouse was a complex building, similar in some ways to a modern leisure centre. A Roman entering it might begin by exercising in the gymnasium area and then pass through a series of rooms, each progressively hotter than the previous one, before jumping into a cold pool for an invigorating plunge. In a culture without soap, cleaning was achieved by covering the body with oil and then using a metal tool called a strigil to scrape off the residue, together with dirt and the uppermost layer of skin.

The bathhouse was one of the most important, and most used, of Roman buildings, a true social centre. People came to exercise, meet friends, and discuss business, as well as to get clean. In Rome itself, there were even bathhouses with libraries. Fascinating information about Roman baths comes from a letter from Seneca, tutor to the emperor Nero, as Dr Janet de Laine of Reading University explains: 'He describes what it is like to live above [a bath] and the noises that he hears. He talks about the noises of people experiencing massage, the different sounds that the masseur makes ... He talks about the noises of the different people who enjoy the baths, particularly jumping into the pool; people who sing at the tops of their voices while enjoying a bath; the sound of sausage sellers. A lot of people simply went there to enjoy themselves.'

Some forts on and near Hadrian's Wall bring us close to the Romans' everyday life. Housesteads is the best example of this. Hundreds of soldiers – originally infantrymen, although the garrison was later were reinforced with cavalry – lived there and their barrack blocks, granaries, headquarters building, what may have been a hospital, and even carved stone latrines, have been excavated. A reconstruction of the latrines shows that they were arranged with a drainage channel beneath to wash waste

▾ Stone carved with a phallus, a common Roman fertility symbol

material into the local stream or river, which was diverted to protect drinking water from contamination. Sponges on sticks were on hand for personal cleaning. And these were communal lavatories – Romans seem to have lacked modern inhibitions about their bodily functions. Presumably business was discussed in the latrines and there was also a social side to them, just as in the baths.

If Roman bathhouses and public lavatories seem alien, many other aspects of Roman life are familiar. Parallels between Roman shopping complexes and modern malls, Roman baths and today's leisure centres spring readily to mind. In addition, Roman concrete, vaulting, and other engineering achievements have left a lasting mark on Western architecture. Although much of Roman culture disappeared when the empire collapsed, Roman features, from arches and mosaics to entire city plans, have influenced British architects from the seventeenth to the twenty-first centuries. Britain's first great builders still have the power to inspire.

Water engineering

In continental Europe, especially in the south where water can be scarce, the Romans built great aqueducts to bring water into their cities. Some of these still stand, vast structures with rows of stone arches, they are even bigger and more impressive than the railway viaducts of the Victorians. Examples such as the Pont du Gard, near Nîmes, France, are among the most justly famous works of Roman engineering.

Britain, with its wet climate, had much less need for elaborate structures like these. Even so, the Romans valued a good supply of water and the convenience of having it delivered where it was needed, and they provided many Romano-British cities with at least some pipes. For example, there

were wooden ones at Colchester and Silchester, earthenware pipes have been discovered at Lincoln, and other settlements such as Leicester, Wroxeter, and Exeter had leats – channels for conveying water. Most of these pipes and channels supplied bath complexes where, more than anywhere, it was important to have a reliable supply of fresh water. There is also evidence that military developments were more likely to be well supplied than the civil settlements that grew up around them. Presumably the Romans were more willing to spend money on the army. Towns and cities in general took much longer to build than forts and no doubt expanded slowly as funds became available.

LATER PARALLELS

Since the seventeenth century architects have been designing classical buildings, many of which were influenced by the buildings of ancient Rome. Indeed, structures like Halifax's Piece Hall of 1792, with its upper order of Tuscan columns, recall Roman architecture. Such columns would have been familiar to Vitruvius, the Roman master architect, who described the classical style and who was copied both throughout the empire and by architects of the eighteenth century.

But the classical style, with its columns and entablatures, derived originally from ancient Greece, is not the essence of Roman building. What the Romans did was take this style and combine it with new constructional techniques such as the use of concrete and the building of vaults and domes, to create radically different spaces. In doing so, they invented typically Roman building types such as the bathhouse.

Today's closest equivalent to the bathhouse is a leisure centre like the Doncaster Dome (1990), designed by architects Faulkner Brown. Its mixture of swimming pools, jacuzzis, gymnasia, saunas, and flumes forms a clear analogue with Roman baths: it is very much a place for socializing and being entertained. And the banded granite masonry (albeit with a functional steel frame) gets quite close to Roman architectural form.

Similarly, shopping malls like the one at Trafford, Manchester, and countless others outside towns all over Britain, remind us that the Romans built covered malls of shops; those in the market complex the emperor Trajan built in Rome are an

▼ Atrium and staircase, Judge Institute of Management Studies, Cambridge, by John Outram.

example. The modern equivalents, enticing on the outside and bold and brash within, evoke an opulence and grandeur with which the Romans would have felt at home.

Malls and leisure centres use modern materials to create large, impressive spaces, just as the Romans used materials that were contemporary to them. Rarely, however, do today's structures have the sense of innovation that made Roman buildings so striking. But at least one major contemporary British architect meets this challenge. One of a number of practitioners who began to capitalize on the new craft skills that were developing during the 1980s, he forged a classical style, but one that put modern materials, from concrete to plywood, to new uses. As a result, the buildings of John Outram have a style quite unlike any other. Outram has

▲ The exterior of Outram's Judge Institute.

▲ The New House,
Wadhurst, Sussex,
by John Outram.

described it as 'taking classicism for a walk'. The bold colours of John Outram's buildings remind us of Roman interior design. He has brought these and his virtuoso use of materials to projects as diverse as a luxurious country house in Sussex and a pumping station in London's Docklands – a combination of lavish living and the utilitarian that would have appealed to the Romans, especially if they had been able to see his polychrome brickwork, brightly painted capitals, and gorgeously varied wall surfaces. His Judge Institute of Management Studies, Cambridge, is one of his most Roman creations.

Outram uses a wide repertoire of wall finishes – brick, marble, and concrete – in a variety of inventive forms. He takes concrete far beyond its functional origins, giving it new incarnations: a favourite is what he calls 'blitzcrete', concrete mixed with fragments of brick and then sliced to give an effect like nougat. This parallels Roman mortar, in which bits of brick or tile were mixed as a binding agent, but it takes the material into new decorative realms. Another effect is produced by engraving spiral patterns on cylindrical concrete beams, what Outram terms 'doodlecrete'. Creative use of materials, a wide range of building types, vibrant colours, interesting spaces – it is a very Roman blend.

chapter two

High and Mighty

THE MEDIEVAL CATHEDRAL BUILDERS

▶ Piers Gough in front of the baptistry window in the modern cathedral at Coventry.

Britain's ancient cathedrals are among our most spectacular buildings. They tower over our major cities, their massive forms seeming to speak of power as well as faith. Their spires and pinnacles make dramatic silhouettes against the sky, and inside their soaring lines lead the eye ever upwards, towards the heavens. Their structures seem amazingly confident considering that the people who produced them had no complex machines or labour-saving power tools, and had to push current technology and materials to the limits to create buildings that stunned and inspired.

The churchmen who ordered the cathedrals to be built had to call on an army of workers: masons, sculptors, painters, stained-glass makers and

craftworkers of all kinds. The result was the largest, most elaborate buildings of the time, bigger and taller than anything that had gone before. The cathedrals were the medieval equivalents of modern skyscrapers, office blocks which break new height records every decade. Just as twentieth-century icons like London's Lloyd's Building or the Canary Wharf Tower made recent headlines, so medieval cathedrals like Durham, just as shockingly new, overwhelmed their contemporaries.

SAXON BEGINNINGS

The story of the cathedrals begins with the Saxons. They ruled England after the departure of the Romans in AD 410, at the time when Christianity was

▾ St John's church, Escomb, County Durham.

spreading through Britain, and built numerous churches. Many were made of wood and have long since perished, and even stone-built Saxon churches are now a rarity. A combination of wear and tear, Viking raids, and Norman rebuilding has seen to that.

The church at Escomb, County Durham, built in the eighth century, shows what many Saxon churches were like. The overall impression is of a building that is very plain – virtually no ornament relieves the flat stone walls, which were originally covered with whitewash. The plan is simple – just a long, narrow nave and a small chancel. A few narrow windows let a little light into the dim interior, which is dominated by a tall chancel arch with a plain, round head that may be from a Roman building. Looking at this small, unadorned building, it seems that architecture has taken several steps back since the heyday of the Romans.

There were larger Saxon churches than this, and others with more complex plans, more ornament, and features such as towers, as well as monasteries and cathedrals. But they have largely vanished. To trace English cathedral-building on the ground, it is necessary to turn to the buildings of the Norman period.

BUILDING ON THE CONQUEST

The Bayeux Tapestry shows that one of the first things that the Normans did when they invaded England in 1066 was build a castle at Hastings, close to the site of William the Conqueror's victory over the Anglo-Saxons. It was nothing grand – a simple wooden structure on an earth mound. But it was followed by scores of others built of stone: massive, thick-walled fortresses that seemed to say, 'We have conquered, and we are here to stay.'

The Normans put 'their' men in charge of the castles. But to take over England completely they had to dominate the Church. The Norman period therefore saw an explosion of church building. Hundreds of parish churches were built or rebuilt and many monasteries were founded, but most important of all were the cathedrals. During the 100 years after

'RELIGIOUS POWER IS DIRECTLY REPRESENTED BY RAW ARCHITECTURAL POWER' the Norman Conquest, sixteen cathedrals were largely rebuilt and another six were started from scratch. William ensured that he appointed the bishops in charge.

This building programme must have entailed a huge investment. Fortunately for the Normans one practice of the medieval Catholic church, the granting of indulgences, made many people want to make a contribution. Alan Piper, tutor in palaeography at Durham University, explains how the system worked: 'When someone made their confession to a priest, the priest said, "I forgive you, but you must perform a penance." The sinner might have to recite the Lord's Prayer fifty times, for example. An indulgence enabled you to do something different from the penance, like come to the cathedral and help build it, or give some stone or timber to the cathedral.' The system of indulgences, which in a sense converted something that seemed not very useful into something very practical, provided vital resources for these large and complex buildings.

ROMANESQUE CATHEDRALS

The style of these new cathedrals derived largely from Roman architecture and is therefore known as Romanesque, although in England it is often referred to simply as Norman. It is a style of thick walls, round-headed arches, and tunnel-like barrel vaults, supported by thick and massive pillars, or piers, which often look like enormous, elongated drums. Like the arches, the windows and doorways have round-headed openings, often beautifully carved.

The buildings were tall for their time, but by the standards of today or even of the later Middle Ages, Norman cathedrals are long, low, and dark. Even the towers are in many cases square and squat. Nevertheless, these structures were bigger than anything seen in England before. Their awesome scale would have made people feel small in God's presence. As statements of power they are just as effective as the Norman castles. Everything about them feels massive.

One of the earliest Norman cathedrals, St Albans (see page 22), which was begun in 1077, shows this massive quality more than most. The arches

▶ Stone faces left after blocks have been removed, showing marks left by plugs and feathers

Quarrying

Using a diamond-toothed saw, a modern quarry worker can slice a 1 tonne block of stone from the rock face in two minutes. In the Middle Ages, without power tools, quarrymen had to work by hand. They looked for natural splits in the stone, then drilled a row of holes into the rock and inserted feathers – two strips of metal – with a metal plug between them. By hammering on each of the plugs in turn they pushed the metal strips apart so that a gap opened up, causing a weakness in the stone and making it split in a straight line. The quarryman then used a large crowbar, a gavelock, to lever the block away from the rock face. He could repeat the process to divide a large block of stone into smaller pieces. At this stage, he might also use a saw to trim the block. None of this was highly skilled labour – the lowliest quarryman could split and cut stone blocks in this way.

Much of the cost of a batch of stones went on moving them to the building site and, as there was little point in transporting superfluous weight, skilled masons and quarrymen were employed at quarries to work stone to a finer finish – often following the instructions of the master mason in charge of the construction. He sent measurements and templates to the quarry, and the stoneworkers followed his instructions carefully, turning out blocks with mouldings, string courses, or other motifs, as required.

Masons working on prestigious buildings might contact far-flung quarries to obtain the best stones. For example, large quantities of stone for buildings in southern England came from quarries at Caen in Normandy. Certain English quarries were also valued for the quality of their stone: Beer in Devon, supplied buildings in London in the fourteenth century, and stone from Portland was also transported widely. The unique Purbeck marble (actually a form of Jurassic limestone that can be polished) travelled far and wide, especially to building sites where there was access to water transport.

are plain and round, the piers huge and square, and there is very little carved decoration. There is a special reason why it is so austere. There is little good building stone in this part of England, and the city is far from the waterways along which good stone could be brought from France. But there was a different sort of 'quarry' nearby: the abandoned city of Verulamium. Most of the cathedral's structure is made of recycled Roman bricks, plastered over to give a smooth surface. This approach gives no scope for carved ornament, and only high up above the building's main arcade are there round columns with simply carved capitals. Even these turn out to have been re-used from an earlier, Saxon building.

The masons of William's time could build more ornately than this, however, as the cathedral at Winchester shows. Here the transepts, started in 1079 and the only surviving parts of the Norman building, show the mason's skill in handling stone.

As in most medieval cathedrals, the interior of the Winchester transept is built in three 'storeys'. At the first level is the arcade, the row of arches leading to the aisle. Above this is the triforium, another row of arches that conceals a gallery above the aisle vault. Higher still is the third level, the clerestory: a row of windows that light the interior from above. The style of masonry at Winchester – the plain arches, the pillars topped with simple, cushion-like capitals, and tall triforium arches that are nearly as large as the arcade below – set the trend for many other cathedrals that were built in the developing Romanesque style.

A DEVELOPING STYLE

Several notable Norman survivals in East Anglia draw on this style. Norwich cathedral preserves much of the work of the period – the nave, transepts, and much of the choir – although the beautiful vaulted roof is a fifteenth-century addition. It also has a decorated Norman tower, to which a spire was added at the same time as the vaults. Nearby, Ely and Peterborough both still have Norman naves (together with many features added in the later Gothic style). Ely is notable for its fine proportions, Peterborough for the lavish use of carved ornament on the arches. All these East Anglian buildings display the typically heavy Norman

▶ Round-headed Norman arches lining the choir and nave at Peterborough cathedral.

construction. However, although the piers in the nave of Peterborough, for example, are enormous, the way they are designed, as clusters of slender shafts like separate miniature columns, reduces the impression of massiveness.

The west of England was another centre of Norman building with several cathedrals and large churches. Gloucester and Hereford cathedrals, together with the abbey at nearby Tewkesbury, have naves with massive, plain piers, quite unlike those of the East Anglian buildings.

Moving and lifting

Getting stones into position on site was as great a challenge as carving them. Walls could be up to 60 metres high and masons therefore needed strong scaffolding. This was made of wood, as it still is in many parts of the world, and had to be able to support the weight of both stone blocks and workers. As John David, a stone mason at Durham, explains: 'Construction of the building probably involved as much timber scaffolding as the amount of stone used ... Imagine the walls, up to two hundred feet high, with scaffolding probably several yards wide on each side, perhaps filling the interior and strong enough to hold blocks of stone weighing up to a ton.' Working in a half-finished cathedral must sometimes have been like hacking a way through a forest.

Many medieval buildings still show holes known as putlog holes after the horizontal scaffolding beams, or putlogs, that fitted into them. The putlogs were lashed to vertical poles with ropes or withies and to make them secure the ropes were tightened by driving in wooden wedges. The scaffolds could be complex structures. On a major building, they came in different sizes for masons working at different heights. Sometimes they had wooden side panels to shelter the workers from the wind, as well as floors, so that the masons could move with ease.

Stones and other items needed for construction were often raised to the tops of scaffolds with a rope and pulley. Baskets and barrels were tied to the end of the rope to transport small stones, tools, and other equipment, while a metal grip on the end of the rope was used for the heavier stones. A great wooden treadwheel, like the one still preserved in the tower of Beverley Minster, Yorkshire, was used when more power was needed to raise big beams and the largest stones, such as the round bosses at the intersections of vaulting ribs. Wheels were built so that they could be moved around more easily as the building progressed and often ended up in cathedral towers, where they were invaluable for raising the bells to the belfry.

DURHAM AND ITS INFLUENCE

The finest of all the Norman cathedrals is Durham, begun in 1093. A perfect site, overlooking a meander of the River Wear, sets off its fortress-like exterior. It abuts on to the nearby castle, presenting a forbidding face to potential invaders from across the Scottish border. Here, more than anywhere, the social and political impact of the early cathedrals is still clear. The building's awesome scale and commanding position make its power obvious. As Alan Piper puts it: 'If you build a cathedral and then put a castle next to it in such a powerful position, the statement is basically: "Don't mess with the chap in charge of this!"'

But it is the interior that makes Durham special. The nave, which survives virtually intact from the Norman period, displays the thick walls, small windows and round arches of the Romanesque style. It is notable for many reasons. The master mason alternated the round, drum-like piers of Gloucester with those, reminiscent of Peterborough, that bear clusters of

▾ Durham's city walls, next to the cathedral's west front.

▲ Reconstruction of the painted decoration on the piers at Durham.

slender shafts. But he developed the design in a striking way. Instead of standing plain as in the western cathedrals, the drum-like piers are adorned with bold, simple carved patterns, intended as the basis for painted decoration. Traces of the paintwork can still be found on some of the stonework, but they only hint at the bright colours and bold patterns that originally covered it, a series of almost garish designs that would have dazzled the eye.

The vault is another feature that marks Durham out from England's other Norman cathedrals. Romanesque naves are usually roofed with timber – their masons often vaulted the side aisles and other small, narrow spaces, but fought shy of the huge technical problems posed by building a stone vault above a high, wide nave. At Durham they took the plunge, aiming to make the entire building out of stone. There were several reasons for this. Stone made the building durable. There was less fire risk than from a timber roof. Above all, completing the whole fabric with stone gave the interior a unity it would not otherwise possess, something that was very important to the Durham masons. At one point during construction they ran out of money, and built the ceiling of the south transept from timber. But as soon as they could they replaced this wooden roof with a stone vault.

Durham's vault also marks a technical advance. Early Norman ceilings were barrel vaults similar to those built by the Romans, great tunnels of rock that needed prodigious amounts of stone in their construction. This made them very heavy and the builders had to use elaborate temporary wooden structures, called centring, to hold up the stone while the mortar was setting. When the mortar had

'IT'S IMPRESSIVE TODAY; 1,000 YEARS AGO IT WOULD HAVE BEEN TRULY AWE-INSPIRING' hardened and the centring was removed the heavy vault created stresses and strains that required the walls supporting it to be massive.

At Durham the masons adopted rib vaulting to overcome some of these problems. This uses a network of stone ribs, infilled with areas of lighter, thinner stone, to thicken the main lines of the vault at the points where the stresses are greatest. This means the rest of the vault can be thinner and the result is a lighter, stronger, more skeletal structure. It is also simpler to build. The ribs are the first elements to be constructed, supported by simple

◀ Durham's choir vault, with its pointed arches.

wooden centring, and when they are in place they act as supports for the wooden shuttering that carries the stone infill. So a rib vault saves money on stone and the wood for the supports, and forms a structure that places less strain on the walls below. It also radically changes the appearance of the ceiling. Dark, tunnel-like barrel vaults are gone, replaced with more soaring, linear forms that lead the eye upwards. From this time onwards, cathedral masons chose a ribbed design whenever they were able to vault their buildings with stone.

The cathedral at Durham was built over forty years, with different builders in charge as time went on. The first master mason, who designed the choir and transepts, knew he was going to vault the ceilings and built this idea into his structure, from the floor up. His columns incorporate slender shafts that rise up to give visible support to the vault. By contrast, the mason in charge of the nave did not use wall shafts on all his piers, so some of his vault ribs rest on corbels – carved stones that stick out from the walls. The design of the nave is less integrated, and less satisfying, as a result.

Nevertheless, Durham cathedral is an astounding building. It must have amazed people when it was first built, all the more so because it was completed in a remarkably short time given the technology of the period. The cathedral's consultant architect, Christopher Downs, explains how this speed was achieved. 'The apparent solidity and massiveness of the construction here at Durham is perhaps slightly misleading. The walls are six or seven feet thick, but are not composed of solid stonework throughout. There is a solid stone face on the inside and a face on the outside, with a rubble-work core between the two.' Building Durham was a huge task, but this type of walling made the process much quicker.

The builders of Durham, like all medieval builders, used lime mortar which takes several decades to set fully hard. Structures could move when masons, working at speed, placed a heavy load on top of the newly laid mortar and this has happened in several places at Durham, where the stones of arches and walls have slipped out of true. But the cathedral still stands, 1,000 years after it was built, a tribute to the skill of the masons who built it.

NORMAN ORNAMENTATION

The masons of Norman England developed a repertoire of decorative motifs that set their work apart from that of their European cousins and which could appear anywhere – around arches, over doorways, above windows. Most popular of all was the chevron or zig-zag, which appears around many of the arches at Durham. Repeating squares, rectangles, or circles, cable or rope designs, and other patterns, were also used, as were repeated fantastic faces with beaks, now known as beakheads.

In the late Norman period, towards the end of the twelfth century, masons in England ran riot with this decoration. A doorway might be surrounded with a number of recessed arches, or orders, each ornamented with chevrons, or different motifs. At Rochester cathedral, for example, the west doorway has five recessed orders, each of which is richly carved, and many small parish churches had two or three orders of ornament around their main doorways. Windows could be treated in the same way, and the decoration could even extend to their sides so that virtually the whole opening was surrounded with rich, deep carving. Where spaces were vaulted, the ribs of the vault were sometimes also carved with chevrons.

The generous area of stone wall in a large Norman church was a challenge to masons and carvers, who were eager to ornament every surface. Towers, west fronts, and other expanses of stonework could be filled with blind arcading – rows of small ornamental arches that had the effect of making the masonry look more delicate. Behind this, however, the walls were still thick and heavy and as the twelfth century went on masons began to experiment with a new, much lighter style.

▾ Zig-zag ornament on Norman arches at Durham.

NEW STRUCTURES

One reason why masons wanted a lighter style was that there were structural problems with Romanesque. A heavy stone vault tends to push the supporting side walls outwards and apart, which can lead to collapse, despite the thick walls of the period. The same thing can happen with towers, and many Norman church towers did indeed fall down in the Middle Ages.

It is also difficult to use round arches for a vault. Their height is always exactly half their width and the wider the space to be vaulted, the higher the arch has to go, the more masonry is needed to build it, the more powerful the outward thrusts – and, again, the greater the chance of collapse. A further problem was that Norman cathedrals, with their small windows, could be very dark. Churchmen wanted lighter buildings. But bigger windows meant weaker walls.

The solution to this problem is already hinted at in Norman buildings like Durham. Although the cathedral is built mainly in the thick-walled Romanesque style, the masons began to use a new structure, the flying buttress, to support the vaults. Flying buttresses, great arched supports that lean against the vault, transfer the outward thrust of the vault into a downward one. At Durham, these are hidden in the gallery above the nave arcade. The next generation of architects would expose them on the outsides of their buildings, and would use them to support vaults in cathedrals with bigger windows and weaker walls.

'CATHEDRALS ARE THE MOST FANTASTICAL BUILDINGS IN THE WORLD'

The pointed arch was another innovation that appeared early, in the vault, at Durham. Pointed arches and flying buttresses transformed our cathedrals. Instead of being structures based on thick, heavy, load-bearing walls, they became skeletal. Because most of the weight of the roof was taken by the buttresses, walls could be much thinner and windows could be made much larger. As a result, churches could be flooded with the coloured light of the sun shining through great stained-glass windows.

THE DAWN OF GOTHIC

The Gothic style was created in France, in the choir of the abbey of Saint-Denis outside Paris, during the 1140s when British builders were still developing and refining their Norman style of building. The head of the abbey, Abbot Suger, was overjoyed with his new choir. He soon began to rebuild the nave in the same style and wrote enthusiastically about how the spaces inside the building were suffused with light. In the following decades the new style spread around the Ile-de-France and Normandy and England's strong links with this part of France meant that Gothic soon spread across the Channel.

The mason's tools

Quarrymen, carvers, and masons used both axes and chisels in their work but, as time went on, and especially after the late twelfth century, the chisel became the more widely used of the two. It was more precise and could be made in a variety of sizes to suit different jobs. Gervase, who wrote an important account of the rebuilding work at Canterbury, described how the men working for master mason William of Sens used chisels to produce much finer work than the earlier carvers who had used axes. Whether they used chisels or axes, medieval masons were capable of the finest work, from simple but carefully cut mouldings to beautiful figurative sculptures. Even items such as roof bosses, so high up in the vault that they can hardly be seen, are frequently carved with telling attention to detail. When work was being produced for the glory of God, it did not matter that mere mortals on the ground were unable to appreciate it fully.

As so often in the history of building, opportunity came on the heels of disaster. In 1174, Canterbury cathedral, seat of the archbishop, was gutted by fire. Plans were immediately made to rebuild it and in the following year a Frenchman, William of Sens, was appointed as architect. William adopted a style very similar to that being used in the cathedrals of the Ile-de-France, and especially Notre-Dame in Paris where building had begun in 1163. He used plain columns (some round, some eight-sided) topped by capitals reminiscent of the classical Corinthian order. His vault is a simple design with ribs supported on shafts that come part way down the walls and seem to rest on the tops of the Corinthian capitals. All these features can be found in early French Gothic cathedrals.

Canterbury also had some uniquely English features. The interior vault was much lower than those in most cathedrals in France and this, combined with the building's great length, makes it seem less towering than its French cousins. Another English feature is the use of Purbeck marble, a dark form of limestone that can be polished to a shiny finish. Both features would be repeated again and again in the English cathedrals of the coming centuries.

After 1175, more and more British builders adopted the Gothic style. They understood the structural benefits of lighter vaults supported by flying buttresses on the outside of a building, and realized how the visual and structural advantages of the style went hand in hand. For example, Gothic buttresses are often topped with tall pinnacles. These both improve the look of the building and have a structural effect, hammering downwards the sideways forces that are acting on the buttress.

Gothic was above all a style that worked for churches and cathedrals. Everything seems to point upwards, dizzying the viewer with an overwhelming impression of height. From the outside, features such as towers and pinnacles point skywards so that the whole building seems to reach towards the heavens. This effect is even more intense inside. Columns are slender, their stone whittled down as much as the masons dared. Arches and high vaults all point upwards directing the eye, and the mind, to higher things.

'EARLY ENGLISH'

Masons in England created a distinctive version of Gothic that was rather different from the work of William of Sens at Canterbury. They replaced his plain columns with piers surrounded by clusters of thin shafts. Pointed arches were often decorated with intricate mouldings. Capitals were carved with a form of stylized foliage called 'stiff leaf'. The Victorians, looking for a label for this style, hit on the term Early English Gothic, or simply 'Early English', and the name has stuck.

Types of tracery

As architects and masons became at ease with the Gothic idiom and what they could achieve within it they developed an increasingly ornate style. An important aspect of this was the development of window tracery – its countless different designs and patterns are one of the most important sources of variety in Gothic cathedrals from the late thirteenth century onwards.

The earliest tracery in English cathedrals consists of a kind of skeletal grid of stone which forms a pattern of circular and pointed forms in the head of the window. Called bar tracery, it was first used in England in the mid-thirteenth century. By about 1300, the English masons who developed the Decorated style were making their tracery more and more intricate, flowing, and organic. In the late fourteenth century, it became more linear. The mullions rise from the window sill to the very top of the window in unbroken vertical lines, so that the shapes in the tracery are closer to rectangular panels. This type of window design marks Perpendicular, the last style of medieval Gothic in England.

Among the notable works of Early English Gothic are the nave at Lincoln (begun after an earthquake damaged the Norman cathedral in 1185); virtually the whole of Salisbury, austere but perfect, and built in a single campaign (starting in 1220) with the exception of the tower and famous spire; the west front of Ripon, with its rows of lancet windows (probably dating from the 1250s); and the north transept at York, another composition with lancet windows of about the same date.

The nave of Wells (probably started in the 1180s) is one of the best examples of Early English and is famed for its elegant piers, each surrounded by twenty-four shafts and topped with vigorously carved stiff-leaf foliage. This carving is interspersed here and there with heads, animals, and figures grouped in miniature scenes.

The sculptors at Wells were also given full scope on the west front, justifiably one of the most famous of all English cathedral fronts. The impression it gives is not structural. Rather, it is like an enormous stone screen, covered with niches, that is spread across the entire front of the building. Each niche was designed to hold a statue, and there were originally 340 of them: prophets, apostles, and other biblical characters, martyrs, confessors, notable churchmen, angels – the whole panoply of Christianity.

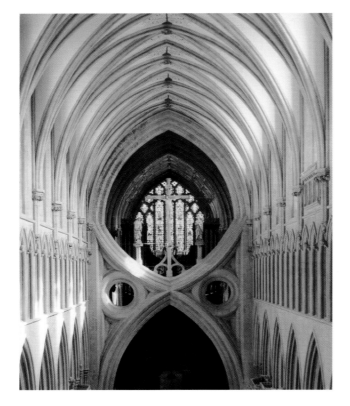

▲ The nave at Wells, showing the Early English arcade and later inverted 'strainer' arch.

Originally, the statues would have been painted like a vast advertising hoarding, one of the boldest spectacles in English art.

Also bold was the decision to heighten the cathedral's central tower in the 1320s: a decision that very nearly led to disaster. The extra mass of stone weighed heavily on the four columns around the crossing below the tower. These began to crack, the foundations moved, and the whole structure could have come tumbling down. To prevent collapse, master mason William Joy built inverted 'strainer' arches at the crossing. These produce an extraordinary effect, with the new arches creating a visual surprise at the end of the vista along the nave. The surprise is compounded by the twin circular openings above the lower arch, like a pair of great eyes, a unique feature in Gothic architecture. Nevertheless, the new arches are integrated with great care into the old ones with matching mouldings and a shape that mirrors the original. However, they are only part of the story. Much of the tower's weight is taken by hidden buttresses.

THE DECORATED STYLE

By the 1320s the masons of Wells had also started work on the new chapter house. This octagonal space is one of the triumphs of English Gothic. Gone is the simple, rather austere idiom of Early English, to be replaced by a filigree style of complex vaults, intricate window tracery, and highly ornamental stonework. It is aptly called the Decorated style.

The chapter house is reached along an older, curving stone stair, and through an opening topped with tracery which seems to herald an exceptional space. And so it proves. The masons were now supremely confident of their ability and what they could achieve with Gothic. From the central pillar, a cluster of thirty-two ribs fans out into the vault. Midway towards the wall, they meet further clusters of ribs. These joins were difficult to resolve architecturally, so the masons marked them with large carved bosses, turning a problem into another decorative feature. Above, in the roof space, the pattern of the vaulting ribs continues with wooden beams that mirror the stone ribs below.

Apart from this bravura vault, the rest of the space is dominated by the windows which fit seamlessly with the ceiling. There is no wall to speak of; it has virtually dissolved into the windows. Below the windows there is simply an arcade, each arch of which forms the seat of one of the chapter members. Nearby, the masons even allowed themselves a touch of humour and included satirical carvings of members of the cathedral staff. Masons still keep up this tradition of humorous portraiture when they restore cathedrals today.

▲ The chapter house vault, Wells cathedral, where ribs converge at a central pillar.

Tracing and carving

As the Gothic style developed, carved details became more and more intricate and the mason's work became more demanding. The flowing, organic curves of window tracery, for example, had to be planned with great care if they were to be successful. As mason John David puts it, 'These windows became an art form in themselves.' Masons scribed the design of the tracery, at full size, into a flat area of plaster floor – a tracing-floor – where it appeared as a series of white lines. They used compasses and careful measurements to ensure that every curve was right. If a mason made a mistake, or when the drawing had been used,

he swept over the lines, effectively dirtying the floor, so that he could start scribing a fresh set of white lines.

When the design was scribed, a carpenter made a series of wooden templates of the curves and mouldings. These were taken to the mason's yard where the patterns were drawn directly on to the face of the stone. Then the mason began to carve, confident that what he was about to produce would fit the master's original design. Modern masons still use the same techniques when restoring ancient buildings – the only difference is in the use of power tools to help with the carving.

'DECORATED' AT ELY

Ely cathedral creates an even more dramatic impression than Wells. Gothic arches and soaring ceilings lift the eye heavenward. The slender shafts work in visual harmony with the vaulting ribs to create a stunning impression of height: buildings like this were the highest structures ever seen in England. At the crossing at Ely is the great octagonal lantern that forms the building's heart, the most daring creation of Gothic building in Britain.

The octagon came about as the result of a disaster. On 12 February 1322, Ely's Norman central tower collapsed taking with it the cathedral's choir together with the adjoining parts of the nave and transepts. Alan of Walsingham was the sacrist of the cathedral, in charge of the building's fabric. He worked with a master mason, whose name was probably John Ramsay, and had the rubble cleared, creating a vast octagonal space with four great arches. In a moment of vision, realizing that the space was too wide to be vaulted in stone, they called in William Hurley who was not a mason but the royal master carpenter.

Hurley created a unique structure, imitating stone vaulting in wood and resting the entire lantern precisely on the pillars below. Hidden away behind the vault are 280 timber beams, many the size of a tree trunk, that hold the structure in place. The whole construction weighs around 400 tonnes, but seems a creation of great lightness. It is one of architecture's great conjuring tricks. The tracery, vaulting ribs, and ornamental carving were all at the cutting-edge of design when they were created, and they are all reproduced perfectly in Hurley's medium. The detail is crisp and precise – even though much of it is over 40 metres above the floor and cannot be seen.

The Lady chapel, built twenty years after the lantern, is the other triumph of the Decorated style at Ely. The Virgin Mary had become an important figure in medieval art and theology, someone who was an intermediary between humans and God, and the custom had developed of building Lady chapels to her. Their customary location was at the east end of a cathedral, beyond the high altar, although the one at Ely is offset to the north of the choir.

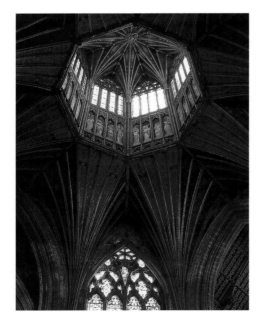

▼ Ely cathedral's octagonal lantern, in which Gothic stonework is imitated in wood.

They are often like separate buildings, architecturally self-contained and almost detached from the rest of the cathedral.

▲ The exterior of the Ely octagon, with the earlier nave and transept on either side.

From the arcading along the wall at ground level to the intricate 'net vault' in the ceiling, Ely's Lady chapel is a triumph of decoration. The arches of the arcade show the ogee, a sinuous double curve that is a typical feature in tracery of the Decorated style. But whereas it is used in two dimensions in window tracery, here it is used in three, curving upwards parallel to the wall and branching out towards the viewer. It is both a daring piece of design and a masterpiece of carving, the stone cut and undercut to produce an almost miraculous delicacy.

Above this arcade, the masons left huge windows to let in as much light as possible. Their flowing tracery seems organic, lending an almost plastic quality to the stone. Higher still, the vault is a dazzling display of ribs, patterned to give the appearance of a constellation of stars.

The features of Ely's Lady chapel – highly ornate carving, complex vaulting, larger windows, sinuous curves – are repeated in other cathedrals, such as Lincoln and Exeter. All were even more highly decorated in the Middle Ages than they are today. The decoration was amplified in the stained glass, wall painting, and embroidered altar cloths. There were even floor tiles with tracery designs baked into their surface. It was a total effect, and one that must have been overwhelming.

The exteriors of Decorated buildings were as elaborate as their interiors. The ballflower, a spherical bloom with incurving petals, was widely used in carved ornamentation, dotted around window and door mouldings. Another feature, which gives Decorated buildings their characteristic ornate outline, is the use of pinnacles decorated with leafy, hook-like forms called crockets.

These slender, encrusted pinnacles often look fragile, and so they are. Builders had to develop a special technology to keep them in place. Instead of simply attaching them to the stones below with mortar, they used a length of metal – lead was popular – or slate to join them. The mason drilled one hole in the pinnacle and another in the stone to which it would be attached, then drilled another, smaller hole in the pinnacle, often in a concealed position at one side. The matching pieces of stone were placed in position and molten lead was poured into the upper hole, from where it ran down into the holes connecting the two stones. The liquid metal filled the holes exactly, before setting very quickly. In this way a precisely fitting connecting piece was created and formed a long-lasting join.

THE PERPENDICULAR STYLE

At court, fashions in art and architecture were ahead of those in the rest of the country and, by the time the Decorated style was established in buildings like Ely and Wells, builders at court were moving on to a new style for the now-vanished St Stephen's Chapel, Westminster, and old St Paul's cathedral. The earliest surviving example of this is the fourteenth-century remodelling of Gloucester cathedral.

The transformation of the building was the result of a tragedy: the murder of Edward II at Berkeley Castle in 1327. He was buried at nearby Gloucester and in 1330 his son, Edward III, decided to turn the Norman cathedral into a kind of royal chapel in memory of his father. The style chosen for this was the avant-garde court style that is now called

▸ Sections of a stained-glass window, held in place on the work table with metal pins.

Glass and glazing

Medieval cathedrals were full of brilliant colour, their stained-glass windows depicting the saints and stories from the Bible – an ideal way, at a time when most people could not read or write, of instructing them in their religion: the priest could point to the windows as he spoke, and his listeners would remember his words much better for having seen the images. People who had donated a window to the cathedral or contributed to the fabric of the building were also depicted.

Stained glass was important in another way. Medieval churchmen believed that a cathedral should be an image of heaven on earth. It should be like a city of God, full of images of the saints, patriarchs, angels, and the son of God himself. Stained-glass windows, along with statues and wall paintings, were a way of populating the city.

Medieval glaziers usually worked with pot-metal, so-called because metallic oxides were added at the glassworks to provide colour. Cobalt was added for blue, copper for greens and yellows. The glazier began by drawing his design, usually directly on the work table. He then took a piece of the glass in the colour he needed, placed it on the table over the relevant part of the design, and traced the required shape on to the glass with chalk. After this he pushed a hot metal rod along the chalk line, cracking the glass to the required shape. Any imperfections could be made good with a plier-like cutting tool called a grozing iron.

Medieval glass-workers exploited their material to the limit and once the glazier had collected all the pieces that made up his design and laid them out on the work table he added extra colours with iron-oxide pigments to pick out facial features, provide shading, and give the images in the windows a vibrant life and complexity.

When all the individual pieces had been painted, they were put into a kiln to 'fix' the details, a process that took two or three days as the temperature had to reach between 600°C and 700°C – and cool down gradually afterwards.

The glazier took the glass pieces out of the kiln, arranged them once more on the work table and used strips of lead to join the sections. Places where one strip met another were carefully soldered together. The completed panel was taken off the table and lifted into its stone frame in the window. A large cathedral window would be made up of many such panels, each of which was either fixed to a groove in the stonework or attached to a network of iron bars, called saddle bars. Even the tiniest openings in the tracery were filled with bright, jewel-like glass to form a composition that could both excite and educate.

One result of this net-like structure of mouldings and mullions is that it enables the walls to be very thin. Masonry and glass can be used in almost similar ways. Windows can increase in size and are usually large, making the buildings very light. The rectangles that continue from the bottom to the top of the windows also make ideal panels for stained-glass workers.

Perpendicular, a word that is appropriately derived from the Latin for plumb line. Its keynote is the use of rectilinear patterns that cover the entire interior. They may start as mouldings covering the walls and continue into the mullions – vertical stone bars – of the windows and their tracery. There is a great emphasis on verticals, hence the name of the style, and this is seen above all in the windows, where the mullions continue right to the top.

Gloucester was not completely rebuilt. Instead, Edward III's masons dismantled part of the building but left some of the old Norman structure behind. As a result there are always glimpses of ancient massive masonry behind the thin-walled construction of the fourteenth century. The two styles do not always fit, but they make a fascinating contrast.

The south transept was the first to be vaulted and, in a way, it formed the prototype for the rest of the remodelling. The Norman turrets and the lower 5 metres or so of the south wall remain, but the rest of the wall was rebuilt to accommodate a great Perpendicular window with mullions running from floor to ceiling. Later parts of the building, such as the choir with its vast east window, develop the style still further. The window, the size of a tennis court, fills the entire east wall and is flanked by diaphanous north and south walls which are little more than thin screens of mullions and tracery, again offering glimpses of the earlier structure beyond. Above it all is a vault of bewildering complexity, a mass of ribs, gilded bosses, and carved angels.

The Lady chapel was built much later, in about 1470. Here the walls have been almost eliminated and the entire space is dominated by the windows, which contain about 325 square metres of glass. The contrast with the oppressive solidity of Durham or the Norman work at Gloucester itself could not be greater.

In the cloister is another ground-breaking feature: the fan vault. The repeating fans of the ceiling are covered with thin ribs that mimic the Perpendicular patterning of the windows and wall panelling. In the fifteenth century, this would have looked outlandishly modern. But the daring is only visual – unlike earlier vault ribs, these are purely decorative and conceal solid masonry. By contrast, the choir contains vaulting ribs that spring from a slender archway that looks as if it could never take their weight. English Gothic could still pull a few surprises.

◁ The fan-vaulted
cloisters at Gloucester.

MODERN CATHEDRALS

Perpendicular was the last phase of medieval Gothic. In the sixteenth century Henry VIII broke with the Church of Rome, and England was soon a Protestant country in which the whole value-system of Gothic architecture – its size, its ornamentation, above all, its images – was frowned upon. Cathedral-building came to a halt.

In the twentieth century, however, more cathedrals have been built than ever before, and different varieties of Christianity have produced different varieties of architecture. The contrast is clear in Liverpool, a city with two cathedrals, one for Anglicans and one for Roman Catholics, both of which were built in the twentieth century.

Early in the century Gothic was still favoured by Anglicans and George Gilbert Scott's enormous Anglican cathedral in Liverpool is the ultimate ecclesi-astical example of the style. Building started in 1902, when Scott won the competition to choose a design, and was completed some seventy-five years later – the last great monument to cathedral Gothic. A building of awesome size, Britain's largest cathedral dominates its surroundings completely. Inside, Scott created a vast interior space beneath the great tower and this forms a central focus quite different from that of a medieval church. Surprisingly, though, the style of Gothic he chose for Liverpool is bulky and brooding. The walls are thick, the windows relatively small, the central tower massive. It is closer to the oppres-sive power of Durham than the delicacy of later Gothic.

By contrast, Liverpool's Roman Catholic cathedral is designed in a wholly twentieth-century idiom and was built, at characteristically modern speed, during the 1960s, to a design by Frederick Gibberd. It is all one vast cone-shaped space, crowned with a lantern of stained glass by John Piper and Patrick Reyntiens. The altar is at the centre and Mass is celebrated 'in the round'. Influenced perhaps by Oscar Niemeyer's cathedral in Brasilia, itself inspired by the crown of thorns, it is a strikingly modern way of creating an awesome space for worship and contemplation.

Coventry cathedral, built from scratch after World War II bombs reduced the medieval church to a shell, is a different story. Soon after the bombing it was decided to keep the remains of the old cathedral, a master-piece of the Perpendicular style, and build a new one next to the ruins. Work began in 1956, and architect Basil Spence went for a free, modern interpretation of the Gothic idiom.

He seems to have been determined to create an impression of lightness. The nave vault lacks the appearance of weight given by its ancient counterparts. The slender columns of the nave taper down to rest on small bronze pins. Spence originally planned to balance the columns on glass balls, but the manufacturers would not guarantee them for 1,000 years. Even without them, the impression is one of magical lightness.

Several features in the building pay homage to the medieval cathedral. The pinkish local stone is in keeping with the ruins and the nave windows, with their walls of stained glass, seem to allude to the Perpendicular style of the old cathedral. What is more, the modern building is full of notable works of art, the sort of striking images that medieval churchmen loved. John Piper's colourful 'creation' window alternates panels of glass and masonry in a burst of light. The end wall is hung with a curtain-like window of clear glass, beautifully etched with angels. At the east end Graham Sutherland's tapestry, the largest in the world, is striking, if somewhat gloomy.

▲ Bronze pin supporting a nave column.

▼ Coventry cathedral: Graham Sutherland's tapestry of Christ in Glory.

Nevertheless, Coventry is an uneasy compromise between ancient and modern idioms, and is somewhat eclipsed by the array of mid-twentieth century artworks it contains. Its architect was making a valiant attempt to reinterpret the ancient style for his own times, but there is no real progression, and little of the structural daring of Gothic – in spite of the tapering columns. It is as if the cathedral was driven more by the need to rebuild Britain after the war than by the faith that inspired the creators of its ancient ancestors.

HEIGHTS AND SPACES

Perhaps the modern equivalents of the great cathedrals are buildings that use huge spaces in interesting ways, and give us new kinds of surprises when we look up at them. Modern builders pride themselves on making taller and taller structures, on breaking height records, just as medieval masons did with their spires. Office towers like London's Canary Wharf, designed by Cesar Pelli, are certainly impressive. They make their marks on city skylines and their steel-and-glass cladding catches the sun and the eye. But do such buildings inspire? Temples to money-making, they represent little that is uplifting apart from their sheer height; little that takes us out of the everyday as the cathedrals of the past were designed to do.

But some modern buildings create great volumes in new ways. A dramatic recent example is London's Imax cinema. Like a Gothic cathedral, glass is its major feature – modern technology allows the entire wall to be made of this, held

▾ London's Imax cinema, with its outer 'skin' of clear glass.

on metal arms – although here the glass is clear and through it passers-by can see an enormous Howard Hodgkin picture. The design of the building allows this image to be changed to revive public interest in the cinema. Within is a huge space which, like a cathedral, is designed to envelop us in imagery, to create a place in which we can be taken beyond our normal working and domestic lives.

Even more striking is Michael Hopkins's Schlumberger Research Laboratories, Cambridge. Hopkins used Teflon-coated fabric and steel to make a large space that is supported with the minimum of structure. Instead of the buttresses of the Middle Ages, which were held together under compression, the roof of the Schlumberger Laboratories is held up by steel guy ropes in tension, like a tent. Where the ropes join the fabric the covering is pulled up in peaks that seem to recall the points of Gothic arches. Inside, light enters the building through the fabric giving the interior a special, ethereal quality. It is unlike the colour-saturated world of stained glass, but light is used in a similarly inventive way. It is in designing buildings like this, temples of art and science which use new materials in interesting, innovative ways, and which create spaces beyond the human scale, that modern architects come closest to their medieval ancestors: the master masons who built their temples to God.

▲ The tented roofs of the Schlumberger Research Laboratories, Cambridge, by Michael Hopkins.

chapter three
The Smoke-filled Room

FROM HALL-HOUSE TO COUNTRY HOUSE

▸ Piers Gough in the hall at Penshurst Place, Kent.

Penshurst Place, Kent, is one of the oldest of the great English country houses. The exterior, with wings and extensions sticking out in different directions, gives the impression of a large house that has expanded and adapted over hundreds of years to meet the needs of its occupants. Inside, in the hall, visitors are in a world not far from that of the great cathedrals. Stone walls are pierced by windows in the Gothic style of about 1290, which fill the room with light. A spectacular roof of chestnut wood stretches upwards, nearly all its timbers straight, a perfect exercise in medieval geometry. High up, great horizontal beams sprout vertical king posts that branch out like trees, their curves giving an organic feel to a structure

otherwise made up of straight lines. This is one of the best preserved of all medieval rooms, as impressive now as when it was built and described as 'the grandest room in the world'.

Several features indicate how it was originally used. The entrance is through a passage concealed from the hall itself by a wooden screen. To the right are the service rooms, such as the kitchen and pantry, and to the left a doorway into the hall. In the hall itself, most of the household sat at long tables arranged along the length of the room on either side of the central hearth. Smoke from the fire rose to a vent in the roof. There was no chimney, but no one seemed to mind. At the far end of the room is a raised dais that marked the position of the high table, where the lord and his family sat. Above the entrance doorway is a gallery where musicians played during banquets.

This hierarchical layout was important in a feudal society, where everyone had to respect the lord, and reflects the fact that this was a multifunctional room. Here the lord both ate and dispensed justice; here his staff both transacted business and, at night, folded up the trestle tables and bedded down on the floor.

As befits such a businesslike space, the materials of the hall – stone, wood, and tiles – are on show. They are functional; there is none of the mystery of a cathedral here. Visitors can take the room in at a glance, from the plain floor tiles to the carved wooden figures – perhaps portraits of the craftsmen who worked here – that hold up the roof.

The hall at Penshurst is the first (or at least, the earliest to survive) in a long line of similar rooms in British country houses. It is the ancestor of reception rooms in some of our greatest buildings. It also relates to much humbler buildings, farmhouses and manor houses dotted all over the country, that were more likely to be made of timber than of stone. These simpler houses both reflect the origins of Penshurst and its ilk, and show how the homes of ordinary people evolved. The buildings are diverse, but all started life as simple, multi-purpose rooms: the halls of England.

MASONRY OR FRAME

Structurally speaking, there are two broad types of building: masonry and frame. In the first, for example a house built of bricks, the solid walls support the weight of the structure. In the second a framework of uprights and horizontals takes the weight and its walls can therefore be thin outer 'skins', like the glass curtain walls of a skyscraper. Alternatively, the spaces between the frame's uprights and horizontals can be filled to produce a wall. This type of structure – a wooden frame with infill – was used in many houses in medieval and Tudor Britain. All the materials (timber, straw for the thatch, clay for the infill) were available in the local natural environment, and construction techniques changed little from the Middle Ages to the seventeenth century.

HALLS OF TIMBER

Throughout the Middle Ages most parts of Britain were well supplied with timber. So for people of ordinary means, the easiest way to build a house was to employ the local carpenter to make a timber frame for the walls and roof. Carpenters were highly skilled and the history of the evolution of the techniques they created is the record of a remarkable structural adventure. As Richard Harris, research director at the Weald and Downland Museum in Sussex, puts it, carpenters were capable of 'transforming the chaos of nature into the precision of culture'.

'THE TIMBER ON SHOW HERE *IS* THE HOUSE. IT'S THE SKELETON THAT HOLDS THE WHOLE THING TOGETHER'

When the carpenter's work was finished other craftsmen filled in the spaces between the timbers to make a solid wall. The most common filling was wattle, a timber basketwork, which was plastered over with a mud-based mixture called daub.

The most widely used form of timber-framed building is based on a simple rectangular framework topped by a series of triangular frames, or trusses, that support the roof. The entire structure rests on a low stone plinth which helps preserve the timbers from rotting. The framework varies considerably, especially in the way the roof timbers are arranged, but the overall pattern of the wall frames is one of repeated rectangles. Between these the carpenter could fit further timbers – diagonals to brace the structure and uprights, or studs, to provide extra support for the wattle-and-daub infill.

Buildings based on this type of timber frame are still common, and vary enormously. The simplest designs have large square or

Working with wood

Richard Harris explains the key role of the carpenter in creating a traditional timber-framed cottage: 'The craftsman who built this house was a carpenter, and he would have been entirely responsible for transforming the trees, which somebody would have given him or he would have bought, into the finished house.' The carpenter had a detailed knowledge of wood – how to select trees for felling, how to prepare timber, and how to put pieces together to make the frame of a building.

More often than not, his chosen material was oak. Of all the English hardwoods, it is strong and long-lasting. It is also less liable to warp and crack, and more resistant to attack from insects, than many other timbers. It is good-looking, a close-grained wood that weathers to a beautiful shade of silver-grey. Other species – elm, chestnut, and sometimes willow – were occasionally used instead if a budget would not run to oak. Another way to economize was to reuse timber from dismantled buildings – humbler houses are often made with wood that has been used at least once before. In the past this re-use has led people to believe that some houses were built of old ship's timbers, but this is unlikely.

For framing, carpenters usually used unseasoned oak as it was much easier to work than the seasoned timber, which was much harder. Unseasoned oak is strong, but prone to warping, so where a precise fit was needed – for example, for doors and shutters – craftsmen chose seasoned timber. In the Middle Ages, woodsmen soaked oak for about a year in fresh water, for example in a millpond, to season it. The natural sap and acid in the wood gradually gave way to water which dried out when the timber was removed from the pond.

An axe was used to fell the trees that had been selected for a building, and the carpenter then hewed the trunk with an axe to make a square beam, or baulk, of timber. He used a saw to cut the baulk into smaller pieces for the separate elements of the frame. Medieval illustrations show carpenters using a two-man saw and trestles to support the wood. Later, the saw pit was developed to give more room to operate the saw. One man could stand on top and guide it, while his assistant stood in the pit.

Carpenters developed a range of different ways of joining timbers, but the mortice and tenon joint was the type used most widely, both in simple cottages and in many larger houses. A projecting piece, or tenon, on one piece of timber fits into a hole, or mortice, in the other. The tenon must fit snugly into the mortice, which entailed precision work with a chisel. The joint was made secure by driving oak pegs through both pieces of timber. By slightly misaligning the holes in the two pieces of timber, carpenters achieved what modern engineers call an interference fit, pulling the tenon into the mortice as the peg was driven in.

When they had finished preparing a piece of timber to form part of a frame, carpenters marked its ends with a number. The piece that joined it was marked in a similar way. This made assembly straightforward as lengths of timber that looked the same but were not identical would not be confused after the journey from the carpenter's yard to the building site. When the pieces arrived at their destination, one method was to put together two whole frames (for example the frames of an entire end wall, together with that of a parallel interior wall) and raise or 'rear' them into position. The frames were then linked with lengthwise timbers which were joined with wooden pegs. The carpenter would need plenty of extra labour for this task, together with ample ropes, pulleys, and wooden scaffolding.

rectangular panels of infill – because wood was more expensive than wattle and daub, the poorer the household the less timber was used. The houses of richer members of the community can look much more spectacular, often with many parallel vertical timbers, or studs, that leave space for tall, narrow panels of infill, a technique known as 'close studding'. Another feature on more expensive houses is an upper storey or 'jetty' that overhangs the lower floor. Jetties were common in town houses. They provide slightly more floor space upstairs, and even more if the building had a second upper storey that was jettied out still further, a feature that is still occasionally seen in the confined space of narrow streets in cities like York. But the main appeal of jetties was probably one of status. In towns, therefore, if a house was built with one wall jettied out, the wall always faced on to the street, for everyone to see. In the country it was usually the higher-status buildings, such as manor houses and large farmhouses, that had jettied upper floors.

The frame and truss method of construction was used in countless houses throughout the Middle Ages and afterwards, and is still used when ancient timber-framed structures are restored. The timber-framed domestic buildings of the Middle Ages were usually very simple. Almost the entire life of the occupants centred on the hall which, just like its grander counterparts in houses like Penshurst, was a multi-purpose room with a central fire.

CRUCK CONSTRUCTION

The cruck was in some ways even more primitive than the timber frame used in the labourer's cottage. It consisted of a matching pair of curved timbers which were joined to form an upside-down V-shape. The carpenter assembled a number of crucks and connected them with lengthwise beams to create the framework of a building.

The construction was in essence fairly simple. Crucks were jointed together on the ground and linked by a horizontal beam (either a collar or a tie-beam) to make an A-shaped frame. These were raised one by one, linked lengthwise with further timbers, and positioned on the ground or a

Wattle and daub

Filling the spaces between timbers with wattle and daub is a highly successful technique which produces walls that look good and, with the right maintenance, last almost indefinitely. An added advantage is that wattle and daub can be made with simple, widely available materials.

The first stage in the process was to make the wattle, a basket-weave panel consisting of fairly stiff wooden uprights interwoven with more pliable material. Thin slices of hazel wood (or sometimes chestnut or oak) were generally chosen for the uprights and were pushed into grooves or holes along the building's horizontal timbers at intervals of around 30 centimetres. Various materials were used to make the basket-weave through and between the staves. The most popular were withies made of hazel or ash sticks from which the bark had been stripped. These were woven between the upright slices of hazel wood to make the basket-weave.

When the panels of wattle were completed they were covered with daub, a mixture of clay, chopped straw, and cow dung. The straw helped the mixture bind and the cow dung provided added plasticity, making the mixture less prone to shrinkage. Other ingredients, such as cow hair, could also be added. It seems that individual craftworkers chose a mix that used local materials and which they found effective. Some of them kept the personal recipes secret and guarded them jealously. The ingredients were mixed together with water, but not too much or the infilling would shrink as it dried.

The daub was spread like plaster on both sides of the wattle, and the final layer was covered with limewash or lime plaster to keep out the rain. The result was a wall that would set rock hard and could last for centuries, yet still allow the air in and out, like a modern breathable material. The only maintenance was renewing the waterproof covering periodically.

The combination of a wooden frame and daub infill creates a pattern of dark lines and lighter rectangles. Nowadays, we are used to thinking of this as 'black and white'. Some medieval buildings probably were black and white from the start. But in many places the look is quite recent, the result of applying bitumen to the wood and painting the plaster white, a fashion that began during the eighteenth and nineteenth centuries. Before then, the colours usually varied. In some areas the oak was left to turn a natural shade of grey, in others the timbers were painted red, as they still are in many places in continental Europe. However they were coloured, the patterns of timber and wattle produced a vibrant design that stood out from the countryside.

low stone wall. The more crucks the carpenter linked together the longer the hall, although the building's width was limited by the length of the timbers making up the crucks. Adding two crucks together to gain extra width was not practical. The resulting 'upside-down W' frame would need a flat roof in the middle, and a flat thatched roof would let in the rain.

Carpenters used crucks for various types of structure: small houses, larger dwellings, and farm buildings such as barns. Two or three were joined to make a simple one-room house; a grander building would require at least five crucks so that there was enough space to partition off the areas at either end – one to act as a service or kitchen area, one as a private room – and leave the middle section as one large open hall.

The scale of building possible with cruck construction is shown in a number of large cruck barns that survive from the Middle Ages. Close relatives of great halls, they are made of the same elements – low stone walls and vast timber roofs held up by the crucks. The barns are totally functional, working buildings: there is no ornament and the structure is clearly visible. One of the finest and largest examples is at Leigh Court, Hereford and Worcestershire. It was built for the Benedictine abbey of Pershore in around 1300 and has no fewer than eleven crucks, encompassing a length of 46 metres and a width of over 10 metres. The great cruck timbers, each made out of a single tree, measure half a metre across in places. They did not all match perfectly, so the carpenter had to modify them to make them fit. Two porches at the side are large enough for carts to enter and are also supported by crucks.

Because crucks are rather simple, it used to be thought that they were the earliest form of timber frame, and that they evolved from the prehistoric habit of linking poles in a V-shape to make a tent-like house. The oldest surviving ones are certainly ancient – thirteenth-century examples are known. But these are far from primitive, and many experts now believe that crucks were invented, perhaps during the twelfth century, for use in quite large, high-status buildings and that other forms of timber framing already existed.

In fact, the fashion for crucks turns out to be based on geography. In general, they are found most commonly in the northern and western parts of England and northern and south-western Wales – broadly, the upland districts of these countries where trees must have been plentiful. Crucks are

◄ Panels of wattle and plastering with daub.

▲ Exterior of the barn at Leigh Court, showing the sweeping, cruck-supported roof.

based on large timbers and there have to be enough of these to make a frame of the required size. In addition, the arms of each cruck must match. In a large building it can be difficult to find matching timbers of sufficient size, but this need not be a major problem in a small one. The timbers may not have to be too massive, and the arms can be matched by cutting a single large tree trunk in two.

Although it is possible to get more use out of smaller crucks by raising them on vertical posts instead of resting them on the ground or a stone plinth, even these require pairs of comparatively large timbers. So in many areas such as the south-eastern regions of Britain where big trees were scarce, builders used straight, rectangular timber frames with roof trusses from a very early period. Even this type of building, however, is limited in width. To increase this, thicker, heavier, and longer timbers were needed, and builders reached a point where such timbers were too heavy to work with – or were simply not available.

'CAN YOU IMAGINE SEARCHING A FOREST TO FIND EIGHTEEN MATCHING CURVED TREES?'

So the width of the buildings was restricted, usually to around 6 metres. As a result, carpenters turned to another type of structure: the aisled framework.

AISLED HALLS

To span greater widths, builders created structures in which the roof was supported by parallel rows of posts: arcade posts. The resulting interiors have a central nave and side aisles, like a church, and so are known as aisled halls.

To construct an aisled hall the builder supported triangular roof trusses of the type used for a frame and truss building on the rows of arcade posts, which also hold up the rafters. These rafters sweep down from the ridge of the roof and cover the aisles on either side of the posts. All sorts of diagonal bracing timbers could be added to make the roof more rigid.

The most magnificent of a number of medieval aisled buildings that survive are the great aisled barns, many of which were built for one or other of the monastic orders. The example at Great Coxwell, Oxfordshire, dates from about 1300 and is one of the most impressive. From the outside it is an imposing structure, its stone roof sloping majestically down to the walls which are pierced only by regularly spaced ventilation holes. Within, it is an awesome space. The tall arcade posts rise from stone pedestals to support the tie beams that span the nave. Diagonal bracing timbers connect the posts with other timbers to give the structure extra strength and rigidity. There is no ornament. This is a working building, designed to provide a vast covered storage space and using the best technology available at the time. Impressive today, it must have been even more sensational when it was built, the high-tech structure of its time.

Wooden aisled halls were used in a variety of ways – for houses, barns, and sometimes even churches in areas where stone was hard to come by. Aisled houses fell out of favour, no doubt because of the obstructions caused by the arcade posts, but the barns lasted and many are still used today for their original purpose. Wherever size mattered most, an aisled building was a favourite choice.

▾ The interior of the aisled barn at Great Coxwell, Oxfordshire.

FARMHOUSES AND MANOR HOUSES

Smaller buildings such as farmhouses used a simpler structure, most commonly the basic rectilinear frame with triangular roof trusses. However, they still left room for experiment and the adventurous use of materials, as is shown by a yeoman farmer's house, hidden in a quiet village in Sussex. It originally had a large open hall with a central fireplace, although this layout gave way to one of chimneys and smaller rooms in Tudor times. What stands out in the building is the use of materials. In addition to the common infill of wattle and daub, the walls were also made with panels of flint and brickwork. The effect is old-fashioned today, but in early times this showy use of different materials would have looked strikingly, even shockingly, modern.

However they were constructed, ancient farmhouses and manor houses usually conformed to a basic plan. The layout can be seen clearly at Bayleaf, a yeoman farmer's house of the early fifteenth century preserved at the Weald and Downland Museum. At the centre was the hall itself, a more modest version of the one at Penshurst. Like its larger counterpart, it was a hierarchical space with a raised dais for the owner at one end. His table was picked out with a coloured cloth and, if the household was wealthy, the

▼ Bayleaf, an early fifteenth-century timber-framed house preserved at the Weald and Downland Museum.

walls behind the table were hung with rich tapestries. By the sixteenth century, when window glass was more common, there might also be a large, full-height window to one side of the dais, throwing light on to the lord and his family. You could have no doubt who was the boss.

Servants and retainers sat on the lower level, lit by the flames from the central hearth. Smoke from the fire rose to a hole in the roof and the atmosphere must have been thick with it. It would have been possible to build a chimney, and many castle towers, where upper rooms prevented the smoke exiting through a hole, had modern-style fireplaces. But people seem to have actually liked smoke. As Richard Harris explains, 'When chimneys were introduced at the end of the sixteenth century, contemporaries complained and said that it was unhealthy to take the smoke out.' In the Middle Ages, people truly lived in a culture of smoke-filled rooms.

Solid infills

Slabs of stone or thin boards were popular alternatives to wattle and daub infills in some areas. They were slotted into grooves in the upright timbers, and usually plastered over so that the finished effect is indistinguishable from wattle and daub.

Brick infill, known as nogging, has been used at least since the fifteenth century and became widely popular, often as a replacement for panels of wattle and daub. Bricks were favoured for their attractive appearance, and the range of different patterns or bonds that could be made, including a herringbone effect. But they are heavy and strain many a timber frame. They are also porous, leading to damp problems and expansion and contraction which in turn create cracks in the wall. Brick infill was never as successful as wattle and daub.

Beyond the high table was a doorway leading to the lord's private room, often known as the solar, where he and his family slept. At the other, public, end of the hall the arrangement was similar to that of grand houses like Penshurst – a screen concealing a passage, with the service rooms beyond. These usually included the pantry, or food-store, and the buttery where the wine and beer were kept. The kitchen might also be here, although in early houses it was often in a detached building to reduce the risk of fire spreading to the main house.

In some ways this type of house would have been uncomfortable by modern standards. For all but the very rich, windows were unglazed. The glass industry was poorly developed in England, and glass was expensive. The Church had access to stained glass, but window glass was little known in houses for most of the Middle Ages. And although windows grew steadily in size in high-status halls through the fifteenth century, with masons adopting the Perpendicular style of tracery that had become fashionable in cathedrals and churches, glass was an expensive luxury for most people until the sixteenth century. Houses therefore had shutters and, probably, thick hangings to reduce draughts and keep out the cold. Little is known about how the shutters and hangings were used – whether people closed them in the worst weather or just at night, or whether they closed all the shutters on one side of a house to keep out a prevailing wind. There is no doubt, however, that cold, draughty houses were the norm.

The same goes for the lack of privacy. In the early Middle Ages even the family of an important lord slept together in one room. It would have been straightforward, and not even that costly, to divide the house into smaller rooms, but individual, personal spaces were not part of the prevailing culture.

CHANGING SPACES

During the sixteenth century fashions began to change and people began increasingly to fit chimneys in their homes. This had a profound effect on the plan of the house and how the domestic spaces were used. There were various ways of installing a chimney, one of the most common of which is illustrated by Pendean, a sixteenth-century farmhouse at the Weald and Downland Museum. Here the chimney is built in the position occupied by the screens in earlier houses, providing the hall with a fireplace. It left room for a small lobby entrance, with the hall on the left and what was originally the service area on the right. This was converted into a new, private room: the parlour. Because it was next to the chimney, it too could have a fireplace

Thatching

Thatch may seem primitive – it must be one of the most ancient of roof coverings – but it also represents an elegant and efficient use of local materials. Properly designed, with a steep pitch and a generous overhang, a thatched roof will quickly throw off rain and snow and give many years of service. Thatch is also lighter than tiles or slates, so the rafters that support it do not need to be as large.

Traditionally, thatchers employed the best roofing material available locally and used plants as diverse as sedge and heather. Today, most thatched roofs are made of straw or reeds. Reeds make the strongest and most durable thatch and the best are Norfolk reeds. Straw, used in the seventeenth-century labourer's cottage shown here, has to be soaked in water before use; the thatcher gathers it together in bundles called yealms to do this. The treatment makes the thatch more flexible. Norfolk reed does not need treating in this way.

Thatchers traditionally begin their work at the bottom of the roof slope, laying the eaves course. It is customary to work from right to left and the thatcher lays the thatch in yealms, fixing them in place either with a thin wooden strip called a sway, or by sewing them to the rafters with twine or a vegetable fibre like old man's beard. Each yealm is secured at its upper end, so that the next, overlapping course of thatch hides the fixing from view.

The yealms are dressed as they are laid, a process that ensures an even layer of thatch and a more durable, weatherproof finish. Straw thatch is dressed by combing it downwards as it is laid, which makes the straws lie in the right direction and removes any loose fragments. Reeds, by contrast, are dressed by hitting the end of the yealm upwards with a tool called a leggett. This tightens the yealm, pushing the reeds together.

The ridge of the roof is the last part to be thatched and is covered by a course which is bent over the apex of the roof to make the ridge watertight. A flexible material such as straw or sedge is best for this. The ridge course is held in place with a ligger, a network of spars – thin strips, usually of hazel wood. The spars often make a pattern of crosses lending a decorative highlight to the apex of the roof. In some parts of the country, the final touch is a sculpture of a bird or beast, made of the same material as the roof, which is placed on the ridge, near the gable.

◁ Thatchers at the Weald and Downland Museum re-roof a timber-framed cottage.

and the lord could retire here to sit and talk. His bedroom was on a floor above the parlour and it too was heated by a fireplace. The service rooms were moved to the opposite end of the house, where the solar had been. At around the same time, much of the cooking activity moved into the hall, with meat roasted on spits in the great fireplace. The plan of the traditional hall house was effectively turned back to front.

This is just one common way of reorganizing the house plan – chimneys could be built in other positions, generating different room layouts, but the overall picture was the same. The arrival of the chimney coincided with social changes – the demand for more privacy, and for a place to sit and talk – that brought about a shift in the focus of the house. Instead of a hall, a multi-purpose living and sleeping space, there were rooms for eating, sitting, and sleeping. It was the end of the old hall house. A recognizably modern plan was emerging.

TOWN HOUSES

All these plans, old and new, had a common feature: a long frontage. This was unsuitable for all but the most lavish houses in towns – where street frontages are expensive – so town houses had to be turned through 90 degrees, to present a narrow facade to the street.

Builders had to decide whether to put the parlour at the front, looking out on the street, or at the rear, next to the garden. Privacy and distance from the noise and smells of the street might suggest the back of the house, but people wanted to present their 'best' room to the world and so the parlour was usually built at the front. Behind it was the living room or hall and, still further back, the service room or kitchen. Because the elegant parlour could not be entered directly from the street, a covered side passage was built

▾ Timber-framed town houses with uprights, or studs, placed close together.

between two houses to give direct access to the rear rooms and provide an indirect route to the parlour.

Although few houses remain with the side passage intact, there are some good examples in Newington Green, London, built in 1658. A passageway leads between two houses and doors half-way along give access to the hall, from which the parlour and kitchen can be reached. The overall layout, with parlour at the front, kitchen at the back, and dining room or hall in between, is preserved in millions of ordinary urban homes today.

WESTMINSTER HALL

The story of how smaller dwellings evolved from hall houses to a more modern plan with bedrooms and parlour is paralleled in the larger houses of the upper classes. These grander buildings went further as lords added more and more rooms, from huge audience chambers to bedrooms for servants, and as builders developed new styles of decoration. In fact, kings and nobles had always found ways of making their halls more magnificent, and had always found master masons and carpenters with the ability to make startling innovations. This is evident in the grandest of all medieval rooms: the royal hall at Westminster.

Westminster Hall was originally built in the 1090s, during the reign of William II, and probably started life as an aisled structure, its roof supported by two rows of wooden pillars. From the beginning it was a multi-purpose building, like any small manorial hall. The first event recorded there is the Whitsun Feast of 1099 and the hall continued to be a regular venue for major seasonal feasts as well as coronation banquets and other important royal events. It was also the home of the medieval law courts and even contained shops. The perfect place to meet anyone of influence in the country, it bustled with activity, especially when the courts were in session. It was where Richard I was crowned in 1189 and where the death warrant of Charles I was signed in 1649. Britain's greatest medieval hall, it was at the centre of national life.

In the 1390s Richard II decided to remodel the hall. He called on two artist-craftsmen who had worked for him for some thirty years: the master mason Henry Yevele and the master carpenter Hugh Herland. Yevele raised the walls, put in huge windows at either end of the hall, and probably replaced the floor.

Herland's was the greater challenge – to create a timber roof that would cover the entire 20-metre width of the building without using supporting pillars.

He solved the problem by combining a hammer-beam design with great arch braces. Both technologies were in widespread use at the time but using the two together was a revolutionary stroke. Hammer beams are like great timber brackets and, with the arch braces, take the weight of the roof covering to the walls. They are like early versions of cantilevers, the structures that carry many modern bridges and other structures which span wide spaces.

Westminster Hall produces its effect immediately, at one blow. The exterior is hardly remarkable, although the great windows and the original spire-like louvres that vented the smoke away from the internal fires must have marked the hall out from the buildings that once surrounded it. But, like the aisled barns, Westminster Hall is about the interior. Here there is no mystery, no sense of changing and opening vistas, as there is in the cathedrals of the same period. Once through the door, the visitor can straight away take in the whole interior, and marvel at the carpentry that makes it possible.

Above all, the scale of the roof impresses. In the 1390s it would have been awesome. The angels that adorn the ends of the hammer beams are taller than a man; the hammer posts are some 6 metres long and each weighs around 3 tonnes. The entire structure probably weighs in the region of 660 tonnes. Lit by candles and the flames of two central fires, it must have overwhelmed Richard II and his court. The hall is still impressive 600 years later, still at the centre of national affairs, and still the place where statesmen like William Gladstone and Winston Churchill lie in state and visiting dignitaries like Nelson Mandela address both Houses of Parliament.

STONE-BUILT MANORS

The walls of Westminster Hall are built of stone and many richer lords often chose this material for their houses. It is durable, and a stone building presents less of a fire risk than a wooden one. These features alone must have been attractive. But stone's most important selling point was that it was a high-status material: it was used for cathedrals, monasteries, and royal houses, and as a result ambitious nobles wanted it for their halls.

In the early fourteenth century, Hugh Despenser, favourite of Edward II, built one of the largest halls of its time at Caerphilly Castle. Over 20 metres in length, it was the work of two of the king's craftsmen: the mason Thomas Bataile and the carpenter William Hurley. There were many smaller stone halls, some of which, like the one at Caerphilly, were incorporated in castles. Others were independent manor houses. Most display the marks of status that stone makes possible: carved mouldings around the doorway, windows with tracery, and other carved details.

Although stone-built halls usually had the same layout as their wooden counterparts there were some interesting variations. As a fireproof material stone was ideal for kitchens and masons were occasionally allowed the scope to make a memorable space of this working room. The finest surviving examples belong to monasteries – the abbot's kitchen at Glastonbury, Somerset, is a large, octagonal building with a stone vaulted roof topped by a central lantern. Few nobles could have run to such extravagance in a room used by their servants, but the fifteenth-century square, tower-like kitchen at Stanton Harcourt, Oxfordshire, with its corners arched to take an eight-sided wooden roof, shows what they could achieve when they tried.

Nobles who could afford such lavish buildings for preparing food usually also wanted more accommodation for themselves and their guests. Wings could be thrown out at right angles to the hall, effectively extending both the private and service areas of the building to create a house that occupied three sides of a courtyard. In some cases, a further wing with a gatehouse was added so that the entire courtyard was enclosed. This was a process of organic growth that often took place over hundreds of years, so it was often the sixteenth century before a family achieved a full, enclosed courtyard. Many a country house, remodelled over the centuries, began its slow evolution in this way.

VIRTUOSO CARPENTRY

In the late fifteenth and early sixteenth centuries members of the gentry, who were growing in power and building up rural estates, began to want bigger, more showy houses. Although many of them could have afforded to build in stone they chose timber instead, probably for two reasons. First, they could build bigger houses for the same amount of money. Second, in the hands of a new generation of master carpenters, the patterns produced by timber framing became showier and more dazzling than ever before. If someone wanted to be noticed, and to be the envy of his neighbours, this was the way to build.

At Rufford Old Hall, Lancashire, begun probably in around 1480, carpenters were given full rein. The framework is a mass of quatrefoils and other ornate patterns. In their modern black-and-white guise they look like the Op Art of the 1960s, but even in their original, more restrained colours they would have been striking. In some places there is so much oak that the expression 'half-timbered' becomes a nonsense. The carpenter and carver have been everywhere you look, elaborating, embellishing, dazzling the eye. In the hall there are more quatrefoils, carved octagonal pillars, and a hammer-beam roof adorned with angels. It may be on a small scale compared with the great roof of Westminster Hall, but it is still a loud statement as if its nouveau riche inhabitants are saying, 'We have arrived'.

Rufford is nowhere more dramatic than in the heavy carved oak screen that stands in the hall. It is movable and spent part of its time concealing the hall's entrance passage, and part nearer the middle of the room shielding the family from the smoke of the central fire. The screen is so theatrical that it may actually have been used as a movable backdrop for plays. Manorial halls made good performance spaces before purpose-built theatres and the owners of Rufford were patrons of actors and musicians.

'ALL ABOUT STYLE AND SHOWING OFF'

There is a tradition that the young Shakespeare, yet to make his name as an actor and writer in London, performed in the hall. A will of 1581 certainly mentions a 'William Shakeshafte' in the context of costumes and theatricals at Rufford, and some scholars believe he was the playwright.

Throughout the late fifteenth and sixteenth centuries, the gentry continued to dazzle their neighbours with virtuoso carpentry, especially in the north-west, a generally poor region where it was as easy to impress with lavish woodwork as

with more costly stone. Houses like Speke Hall, Merseyside (1490) and Churche's Mansion, Nantwich, Cheshire (1577) continued the tradition, casting aside restraint and modesty.

▲ Stokesay Castle, Shropshire, a structure combining wooden and stone construction.

LITTLE MORETON HALL

Perhaps the most magnificent of all the black-and-white houses is Little Moreton Hall, a prodigy of woodwork in the Cheshire countryside. Like many of Britain's greatest buildings, it changed and grew over the years. It began as a hall house in the late fifteenth century and over the next 100 or so years the Moreton family modified the building, making it larger, growing it into a courtyard structure, rendering it more convenient and more fashionable. In the process, they produced the riot of patterning that makes it the most spectacular of all timber-framed houses. Even though the original timbers would have been their natural weathered grey, with yellow ochre infill, the effect would have been dazzling.

Two of the Moreton family's alterations stand out. In 1559 the house was given bigger, more elaborate windows. Both owner and craftsman were so proud of the work that they added an inscription above the great bays in the courtyard: 'God is Al in Al Thing: This windous Whire made by William Moreton in the yeare of our Lorde M.D.LIX. Richard Dale Carpeder [carpenter] made thies windous by the grac of God.' Their pride is not surprising. For centuries, glass had been a luxury beyond the means of all but the richest families and the Church and most medieval halls had wind holes rather than proper windows. But here were a pair of double-height bay windows, each made up of dozens of tiny pieces of glass leaded together in wild patterns. Striking from the outside, they are even more impressive within, flooding the hall and drawing room with light.

The Moretons' second major alteration was a daring afterthought. Extending their house to provide a new south wing, with guest accommodation and a gatehouse, the Moretons decided to add an extra storey. Here they built a new type of room, a long gallery that ran the length of the south wing and protruded from the original roof line. Long galleries were the latest fashion. They were intended for exercise, spaces in which Elizabethan ladies and gentlemen could walk and talk without getting their elaborate clothes muddy. They were extravagant, luxury rooms, like exercise pools in the homes of the rich today.

The Moretons' long gallery seems to totter at the top of their house, looking as if it could fall off at any moment. It is the most daring of designs and the rows of expensive windows, and the timber patterned in quatrefoils, quarter circles, and diagonals make it even more ostentatious. The ostentation continues inside the gallery. The famiy fitted plaster friezes at either end, illustrated with allegorical figures of Fortune and Destiny copied from a mathematical treatise of 1556. The Moretons, rich tax-collectors and friends of the king, had to have the latest fashion, and had to show it.

PRODIGY HOUSES

If a newly wealthy family in a poor county could create a fantasy like Little Moreton, how did the super-rich and the aristocracy of Elizabethan England live and build? A look at their surviving houses answers this question. These

▲ Little Moreton Hall from the south, showing the windows of the long gallery.

◀ Bay windows at Little Moreton Hall.

extraordinary buildings have rightly been dubbed 'prodigy houses'. Their huge windows, fine stonework, intricate decoration, and magical skylines enlivened with turrets, finials, and obelisks had never been seen before in British building.

Longleat, Wiltshire, with its mass of bay windows; Woolaton, Nottingham, dominated by its enormous lantern tower; Burghley, Leicestershire, topped with a stone spire. These are three of the most famous examples of prodigy houses, but dozens of lesser ones were constructed in a rush of country-house building between 1560 and 1620.

How did they come to be built? One answer lies in the character and behaviour of the queen herself. Elizabeth I was not a great builder. A lover of princely magnificence, she preferred to take her court on tour, visiting her most prominent courtiers and bearding them in their own dens. Their response was to build country houses that provided a worthy setting for their monarch – who saved herself the money they had felt obliged to squander. In many ways the greatest of all of these houses was Hardwick Hall, a glittering composition of windows and turrets built for Elizabeth, Countess of Shrewsbury, 'Bess of Hardwick', one of the most formidable women in the land.

HARDWICK HALL

Bess of Hardwick was as remarkable a woman as her sovereign. She amassed a huge fortune by marrying four wealthy husbands and lavished it on her house, which she rebuilt twice. For the second rebuilding she employed Robert Smythson, the greatest country house architect of the time and together they covered the facades of Hardwick with windows (Bess owned her own glass works, so could stand the expense). The windows are aligned, in the most up-to-date manner of the time, in perfect symmetry, even though the interior is far from symmetrical and many of the windows conceal staircases and chimneys. There is little surface ornament, and the row of columns on the ground floor is the only intrusion of classical architecture, a fashion that would soon sweep the country. However, Bess made her decorative mark high on the parapet – her initials, surrounded by ornate strapwork, are silhouetted in stone against the sky.

▶ Hardwick Hall: turrets topped by the initials of Elizabeth Shrewsbury, 'Bess of Hardwick'.

The interior of Hardwick is a surprising mixture of old and new. There is a long gallery, as fashion dictated, which runs the entire length of the house and seems to have been designed around a set of tapestries that Bess bought while the house was being rebuilt. The gallery is lit by many large windows, as one would expect in a house of this size. There is a traditional hall, but it is modest in size. Although a fireplace provides smokeless heat, the hall was not intended to be used in the old way. It was more a place in which to arrive than the multi-purpose room of the Middle Ages.

'A STONKING BLOODY-MINDED CREATION'

After the hall, the revolution in interior space that Hardwick represents becomes clear. A stone staircase ascends, winding its way through the house, pausing at landings that open up views of tapestries, friezes, and vistas into rooms. It forms a dramatic series of spaces that seems to promise an important destination. And so it proves. At the top is Bess's high great chamber, the true reception room, one of the most memorable of all English interiors, and the greatest surprise in the house.

The entrance is through a door beneath a frieze showing the Shrewsbury coat of arms and one is immediately struck by the large, well-proportioned space with floor-to-ceiling windows which cast shadows of their diamond panes on the floor. The room is hung with Brussels tapestries which illustrate the story of Ulysses, and above them is a delicately coloured plaster frieze of another mythological subject: Diana and her hunters. Here, among the characters of Greek mythology, sat the legendary Bess, receiving visitors and overawing them with the magnificence of her chamber and her person.

'A REVOLUTION IN INTERIOR SPACE'

Although the room was first and foremost a glamorous reception room, it was also comfortable enough to be the family sitting room where people could relax and talk. In all its splendour, this chamber and the rooms around it mark the decisive shift away from the hall to the multiroom house. Hardwick Hall was a hall in name only.

Buildings like Hardwick and the other Elizabethan 'prodigy houses' foreshadowed a coming trend. Increasingly, architects, not the master

craftsmen, were becoming the creative force in the world of house-building. In the following centuries, they were to create whole design vocabularies with which they could amaze their patrons. Hardwick was a hint of things to come.

▲ Hardwick Hall: the High Great Chamber.

MODERN PARALLELS

Many people today feel a deep nostalgia for the timber-framed houses of the Tudor and medieval periods. All too often, this is expressed in modern, mock-Tudor structures that have little to do with ancient timber-framed halls. In a medieval hall the weight of the building is taken by the timber frame. But a mock-Tudor house is built of bricks or concrete blocks – the wooden 'frame' is added afterwards on the outside and plays no structural role. Nor is its interior anything like the inside of a Tudor or medieval house. There are many small rooms rather than a few large ones, and they are entered from a narrow passage-like hallway rather than the open hall of earlier centuries. The plan that evolved for town houses in the seventeenth century has had fake Tudor beams and ersatz cosiness grafted on to it. It is hardly architecture at all.

Although few of the craft skills employed in traditional timber-framed building are used on mock-Tudor suburban houses they have not died. A visit to properties like Little Moreton or one of the many English villages that still have ancient half-timbered houses, will show carpenters using

▸ Modern 'mock-Tudor' houses.

time-honoured techniques on repair and maintenance projects. The conservation movement, and modern planning laws, mean they will never be out of a job.

Occasionally these craftworkers get the chance to build something from new. A famous example is the Globe Theatre on London's Bankside. It is a reconstruction, as close as is practically possible to the original given modern safety regulations and audience needs, of Shakespeare's Globe. Its structure – jointed oak frame, wattle and daub infill, and thatched roof – shows what is still possible with the old technology and it comes as a shock to see it among the narrow streets and converted warehouses of Bankside. Shocking as it is, however, the Globe is hardly a modern building.

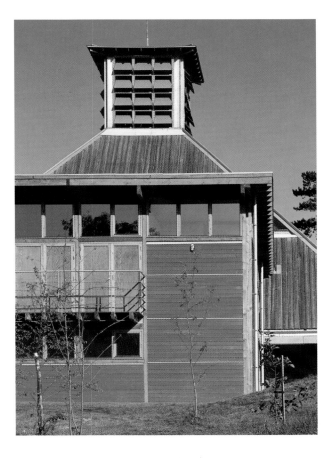

▾ The Olivier Theatre, Bedales School, by Fielden Clegg.

THE OLIVIER THEATRE

One convincing approach to modern timber-framed building is the recent Olivier Theatre at Bedales School, Hampshire, designed by the architects Fielden Clegg and completed in 1996. A plain, barn-like exterior, with a striking, 18-metre high chimney, conceals an open auditorium with a stage that can easily be adjusted for proscenium, thrust-stage, or in-the-round performances. The frame of English oak and cladding of Douglas fir and English larch are visible, but there are modern additions. Steel is used widely, for example in supporting the balconies. This extra support means that fewer oak posts are needed, and sightlines from the seats below the balconies are preserved. Many of the joints that link the timbers are the traditional, efficient ones used by early carpenters, but where tension forces in large spans are too great for the joints, steel ties and plates have been introduced. This combination of techniques shows how the architects have used the craft skills of the past in combination with modern technology to make statements about the present.

One of these statements is to do with ecology. Timber is a renewable resource, and the building is admirably low-energy. Ventilation, for example, is provided by a natural system. A labyrinth of concrete blocks beneath the floor stores cool air, which is drawn up through the auditorium by the tall chimney stack. Even a packed performance on a hot summer evening is made bearable by this system.

In addition, the theatre fits well into its surroundings, and into a school with a tradition of timber-framed building including a famous library designed by Arts and Crafts architect Ernest Gimson. One effect of this, however, is to make it rather modest. It is a far cry from the extravagance of the timber framing of houses like Little Moreton Hall.

HIGH-TECH SOLUTIONS

▾ The Glass Building, north London, by architects CZWG.

For many designers, the architecture of High-tech has become the modern equivalent of the old-fashioned timber frame. The style may seem superficially different, but many architects are intrigued by the possibilities of the old joints and frameworks. Some of Norman Foster's earliest published drawings, for example, are of traditional timber jointing. Like medieval timber work, High-tech is a style of frameworks and skeletons, of strong lines and joints which are celebrated for their own sake. It is an architecture that lends itself well to prefabrication. It is an idiom in which the frame is more important than the infill. Richard Rogers's Channel Four Building in London is a beautiful example, in which steel frameworks – together with glass and timber – create a dramatic, triple-height gathering space. This foyer is designed to remind the visitor of the large open spaces of a television studio, and to be a place where the media meet the people. Shiningly modern as it is, it has something about it of the public spaces created by medieval halls.

If the Channel Four Building gets close to the halls of England in its creation of space, so does the Glass Building, recently unveiled in Camden, London, by Piers Gough's firm, CZWG. The spaces here reflect the way in which many city-dwellers in the last ten to twenty years have looked for more open-plan, free-form interiors in their houses and apartments. The architects have provided wide open adaptable spaces, galleried areas, and a minimum of partitions or other interruptions in the apartment interiors. Residents can move in and adapt the spaces to their own lifestyles. In doing so, they may create something that, without the smoke or draughts of the Middle Ages, provides a modern parallel to the open-plan, multifunctional halls of England.

◂ Channel 4 Building, London, by Richard Rogers.

chapter four

Built to Order

THE CLASSICAL STYLE AND THE GEORGIAN HOUSE

In the early seventeenth century, there was a revolution in British architecture. The classical style, based on the architecture of Greece and Rome and influenced by the Renaissance in Italy, finally came to England. During the next 200 years it would transform the way the British designed and built their homes. Every type of house, from royal palace to the humblest city terrace, was touched in some way by the new style. Architects everywhere adopted it and no builder could ignore it. It transformed Britain's towns – and many parts of the countryside too.

     The man who brought classical architecture to Britain was Inigo Jones, who had begun as the stage designer of the masques put on to entertain the court of James I. In 1613, Jones rose to become surveyor of the king's works,

▶ Piers Gough at
Holkham Hall, Norfolk.

'FROM THIS KIT OF PARTS GLEANED FROM ANTIQUITY, PALLADIO SHOWED HOW TO CREATE PERFECT CLASSICAL BUILDINGS'

responsible for all the royal buildings. Twice in the early seventeenth century, he visited Italy, where he had a chance to study at first hand the monuments of ancient Rome. He used as his guide the *Four Books of Architecture* by Italian architect Andrea Palladio, which was to become, and remains one of the most influential works on the subject ever published.

The drawings and writings of Palladio provided the blueprints for a style that countless others would copy. First published in their complete form in 1570, the *Four Books* cover four separate areas: the classical orders, rules, and elements; the design of country villas and town houses; public works; and the buildings of ancient Rome. It could therefore be used as a complete architect's source book, a set of standard designs which could be adapted to suit everything from modest town houses to vast mansions.

Jones looked at the Roman buildings illustrated by the Italian architect, studied them carefully, and made notes in his copy of the *Four Books* as he went along. He noted how the details of one building varied from those of another, and jotted down extra information that Palladio had missed out. It was probably the first time that someone from England had studied ancient classical buildings in such depth. He also had the chance to see the recent buildings of the Italian Renaissance and to discuss technical questions with Vicenzo Scamozzi, Palladio's colleague. As Simon Thurley, director of the Museum of London, puts it, Inigo Jones was 'the first person in Britain to really understand the principles of both classical architecture and Renaissance architecture'.

THE BANQUETING HOUSE

Back in England, Jones had an ideal chance to put his ideas and observations to practical use. In 1619 work was begun on building a new royal banqueting house in London's Whitehall. By the following year this amazing building had risen among the half-timbered sprawl of Jacobean London. The new classical style had finally arrived.

With its classical columns, symmetrical facade, and rectangular windows, the Banqueting House must have looked totally unlike everything around it.

The building's originality and richness were emphasized by the use of three stones of different colours to pick out the details. And these details show that Jones had studied his sources. Classical buildings are based on the orders, rules that define separate sets of design details and give the architect standard ways of designing the key features of a classical building. The proportions of the columns, the style of the capitals at their tops, and the arrangement of the entablature (the masonry above the columns) are all laid down.

The orders are easily recognized by the different styles of their capitals. The ancient Greeks had three orders: Doric with its plain capitals, Ionic with its scroll shapes, and Corinthian with its capitals smothered in acanthus leaves. Renaissance architects like Jones based their work on the buildings of ancient Rome, so they could also choose two further orders developed by the Romans: Tuscan, which was very plain and similar to Doric, and Composite, with capitals that looked like a combination of Ionic and Corinthian. They developed a hierarchy of orders, for example with Corinthian at the top, and Ionic and Doric lower down. The facade of the Banqueting House, with Corinthian above Ionic columns, respects this hierarchy.

Within the building there is the same hierarchy, with Ionic columns supporting the balconies from which spectators looked down on the scene below and Corinthian to hold up the elaborate ceiling. Today, this magnificent ceiling, with its nine allegorical paintings by Peter Paul Rubens, dominates the banqueting hall. As Simon Thurley puts it, Jones and Rubens, 'the two greatest minds in England at the time', collaborated on this interior to produce 'a great celebration of the Stuart dynasty'. In Rubens's paintings ambassadors approach the royal throne, the virtues and benefits of Stuart rule are personified, and the seated figure of James I looks out from the central oval. During the royal banquets and entertainments held below, there was a similar focus on the real flesh-and-blood king. The royal set-designer had created the perfect stage for the monarchy.

In doing so, Jones adapted the style of Palladio and the Romans. Proportions were important both to him and his predecessors and in theory, the Banqueting House has those of a double cube, one of the most admired layouts for a Renaissance room. In fact, because the site was not big enough, the building is not quite a double cube. Much more dramatically different from the Italian norm was the way the interior was decorated in the seventeenth century. Most of the windows were blocked out and the walls were hung with huge tapestries. The effect must have been rather plush, and a world away from the chaste interiors of Palladio's north Italian villas whose style inspired Jones. It is a very British form of classicism.

'THE PROTOTYPE MODEL OF ENGLISH CLASSICISM'

▾ Interior of the Banqueting Hall, showing the tapestries as they appeared in the seventeenth century.

In the 1620s few British people had seen anything like the Banqueting House. One English writer, seeing it popping up among the Jacobean chaos of the rest of James's Whitehall Palace, commented that it was 'too faire and nothing suitable to the rest of the house'. Classicism was shocking, but Jones continued to build in the style, creating such masterpieces as the Queen's House at Greenwich (begun before the Banqueting House but finished in 1635), the Royal Chapel at St James's Palace (1623–7), and St Paul's Covent Garden (1631).

As he worked, Jones continued to adapt the classical style and developed designs for such features as chimney pieces, which play a minor role in Palladio's designs and are not depicted in his drawings. Palladio, in the Italian manner, put fireplaces on outer walls, whereas Jones moved them to inner walls where they could be placed back to back. This affected the way the windows could be arranged on outer walls, which had an impact on the proportions of the design. With adaptations like these, English classicism developed along slightly different lines from its Italian counterpart. The orders and the basic rules of proportion, however, remained.

BAROQUE INTERLUDE

In spite of Jones's pioneering work, the style he adapted from Palladio and the Romans did not catch on quickly in England. This was partly because a new generation of architects, headed by Christopher Wren and his pupil Nicholas Hawksmoor, started to build in a different syle. Both were heavily influenced by the architecture of Italy. They still used the orders, together with other Renaissance details like square-headed windows and classical vaults, but favoured the more extravagant Baroque style. An architecture of sinuous curves and lavish ornament, it was a far cry from the austerity of Jones's work. Again, it adapted Italian models in a particularly English way. The famous steeples of Wren's city churches, built in London after the great fire of 1666, combine elements from other architectural styles – such as Gothic spires and lanterns – and dress them up in classical clothing. Hawksmoor worked in a similar fashion, incorporating elements such as obelisks into his massive, theatrical churches. Architecture seemed to be veering further and further away from the disciplined style of Inigo Jones.

ENGLISH PALLADIANISM: CHISWICK HOUSE

By the 1720s, buildings that would change this trend were appearing. Among the first was a large house at Wanstead, Essex, designed by Colen Campbell in the years leading up to 1720. It was to be a model for many large country houses built over the next few years. Campbell also designed smaller country houses influenced by the style of Palladio's villas in northern Italy. The most distinctive of these is Mereworth Castle, Kent (1723–5), a compact, square house with a columned portico and a central dome, modelled closely on Palladio's Villa Capra near Vicenza. The same villa inspired the most influential of all these Palladian buildings: Chiswick House, Lord Burlington's classical masterpiece on the outskirts of London.

'CHISWICK WAS THE SHAPE OF THINGS TO COME'

Rigorous in its order, striking in its pale purity, Chiswick must have looked totally alien in 1730 – indeed in many ways it still does today. Lord Burlington created the effect: he was deeply interested in classical culture and, unusually for a nobleman at this time, designed the house himself. As a young man he had gone, like many of his contemporaries, on the grand tour of Europe. He studied the classical buildings of Italy and brought trunkloads of art home with him. Chiswick House was built as an elaborate gallery to house these treasures.

▸ Chiswick House, showing the dome, portico, and rusticated lower storey.

At the entrance to the house stand statues of Palladio and Inigo Jones. For Burlington respected his English predecessor as well as his Italian model. His building is a refined vision of Italy seen over the shoulders of Jones, who is looking in turn over the shoulders of Palladio. It is a refinement of a refinement of a refinement.

The rooms on the main floor are arranged around a central octagonal hall, each with its own perfect geometrical shape and style. One follows the next in a sequence designed to vary the pace and delight the eye – square, double square, and circular plans are all used, together with a long room with semicircular, apsidal ends. Niches designed for the statues in Burlington's collection punctuate the walls, and vistas open up of paintings and of fireplaces based on some of Jones's designs. The house is austere, but the austerity is tempered by the art displayed there.

Chiswick's inventive sequence of different-shaped rooms was influential. So was its exterior. From the garden it can be seen that the main rooms are raised up on the first floor – what the Italians called the *piano nobile*. The lower storey was given the appearance of rough, unhewn masonry, an effect known as rustication. The surfaces of the walls look as if they have been eaten into by a worm-like action, a finish referred to as vermiculation. The lower storey also has smaller windows than those of the first floor. This different treatment expresses the fact that it is the service area of the house, which the educated observer of the time would expect to be given a different, less elegant look than the state rooms above.

The facades at Chiswick are symmetrical and rather severe. The triple windows, known as Venetian windows, have a central, arched-headed opening which is taller than those on either side. The walls, built of brick, are rendered to imitate the pale colour of Palladio's villas in northern Italy. One hundred years after Inigo Jones introduced Palladio in London the Palladian style, still shocking enough in this leafy, out-of-town context, had truly arrived.

'LIKE NO BUILDING SEEN BEFORE IN BRITAIN'

▾ Three-light Venetian window, a typical Palladian feature.

THE PALLADIAN INFLUENCE

Chiswick House and the Palladian style were widely copied for several reasons. First, Palladianism had an excellent publicist in Colen Campbell, who not only designed many of the buildings but also published his drawings in a lavish series of volumes called *Vitruvius Britannicus*. Meticulous and beautifully produced, this publication was aimed at rich patrons and architects and illustrated the masterpieces of the British Palladian style. Other volumes of designs also appeared throughout the first half of the eighteenth century, to give ambitious country-house owners something to aspire to.

A second reason for the spread of Palladianism was Burlington's personality. Although he was his own architect at Chiswick, he gathered a creative circle of architects and designers around him. Campbell was a member of the Burlington circle, as were Henry Flitcroft and Roger Morris, both of whom designed houses and villas in the Palladian style. Perhaps the greatest of all these men was William Kent, who began as a painter and interior designer – he had worked on the decoration at Chiswick House – and became an architect of Palladian country houses. He led the transformation of English gardens from strict formality to a more open, landscaped approach.

Burlington fostered the careers of all the members of his circle, using his power to recommend them to other patrons, and discussing with them their work and the principles of the Palladian style. This was true, most of all, of Kent. He and Burlington corresponded throughout their lives, the nobleman no doubt refreshed by the professional architect's enthusiasm and lack of formality. The two were more like friends than master and servant.

In the discussions of the Burlington circle and the books published by its members and their associates, a vocabulary of the Palladian style emerged. Certain room shapes and proportions were recognized as being attractive and harmonious. For example, cubes, double cubes, and one-and-a-half cubes were seen as basic proportions, and variations were played on these. Rules were also evolved for the size of domes and other features.

Most important of all were the orders, the basic styles for columns and the lintels they support. The Palladians gave each order its own character and significance. Doric, visually simple, was said to be masculine and strong. Ionic, with its scroll-shaped capitals, was said to represent wisdom. The more elaborate Corinthian was linked with femininity and beauty. These features could be adapted to buildings of any size from a small town house to the largest country mansion.

HOLKHAM HALL

The grandest Palladian architecture of all can be seen at Holkham Hall, Norfolk, the house built for Thomas Coke, Earl of Leicester, and finished, after a design and building period of some twenty-five years, in 1762. Protruding from the agricultural land that brought the Coke family their money, Holkham has both magnificence and simplicity. The central block of the house is a mass of raw umber brick, the Norfolk brick-maker's best approximation to the material of many palaces in Renaissance Rome. In the centre is a portico held up by six tall columns. To the left and right are short turrets with pyramid-shaped roofs. A row of windows, a rusticated lower storey, and a pair of smaller wings to the left and right complete the picture. This simple, unfussy design is the work of William Kent.

'THE TOP-OF-THE-RANGE VERSION OF THE TOP MARQUE OF BRITISH CLASSICISM'

The elegance of Holkham's exterior clearly owes much to Burlington's influence. Inside the house, it is a different story. Coke, like many aristocrats in the eighteenth century, had been on the grand tour. Indeed, his tour was grander than most. He took his Oxford tutor and his agent, and spent six years in Europe where, with the help of his agent, he bought art on a large scale, especially in Italy. The interiors of Holkham were intended to show off the paintings, sculptures, books, and other items that he had acquired, and the central block of the house is like one large art gallery.

From the entrance hall all the way through the house the note is one of sumptuous materials, strong colours, and dramatic forms. The hall itself, modelled on Roman baths, is dominated by curving rows of Ionic columns made of mottled brown Derbyshire alabaster. Above these a gilded frieze leads the eye to the extraordinary ceiling. This is coffered – punctuated with a regular grid of square, inset panels – and curves at the back to a semicircle. Broad stairs lead to the *piano nobile*, where the largest rooms are arranged.

Bricks

Bricks use clay, a widely available material, are easy to make, and because of their small size and variable colour can be used in many different ways and for many different effects. During the Georgian period they became not only basic to the building industry, but also fashion items. To produce the rather sombre-coloured bricks prized by Palladian architects, brick-makers used clay which contained plenty of lime. This clay was found mainly in the southeastern half of Britain. But as time went on, builders experimented with brighter effects. They added mineral salts to make them in different colours, enabling builders to create polychrome patterned brickwork. Bricks could also be moulded or cut to make a variety of shapes: mouldings around doorways, arches over windows and doors, cornices along the tops of buildings, and ornamental balustrades could all be made out of specially shaped bricks. What is more, brick-makers knew how to cut their material accurately, so bricks were ideal where precision was needed.

Peter Minter, managing director of Bulmer Brick and Tile, a company that makes handmade bricks, says they make bricks 'in almost the same way as the Georgians did. Very little has changed in this works over the hundreds of years.' The brick-makers begin by digging the clay, usually in autumn so that the material can be left to weather over the winter. Weathering is important because the action of rain and frost encourages many mineral salts to leach out of the clay and if it is fully weathered there is less chance of the salts coming out of the finished bricks and leaving white stains on a wall. Two days before the clay is needed it is left to soak in water. The mixture of water and clay is then put into a pug mill, which is like a large food processor. When it has been mixed into a paste it is ready for the brick-maker.

The maker adds sand to the wooden brick mould as a releasing agent, then throws clay into the mould, removes any excess from the top, and removes the mould to reveal a brick-shaped piece of damp clay. This is left to dry in the fresh air before being taken to the kiln for firing.

Bricks spend several days in the kiln, which heats up and cools down gradually. The amount of heat and the length of time for which the bricks are fired is another factor that affects the finished appearance, and an experienced brick-maker will have a good idea of how long they should stay in the kiln to get the colour that is required. But there is always an element of uncertainty.

Many large, more expensive houses made from brick had finishing touches – window surrounds, quoins (corner stones) and the like – of stone. But fine details can also be produced by cutting finished bricks to make different shapes, such as ornamental mouldings or the separate sections (voussoirs) of an arch. The latter could involve drawing out the entire arch and indicating the shape of each brick. A saw is used to cut individual bricks to the required shape, and they are then rubbed smooth with a slab of stone or another brick until precisely the right size, shape, and finish is achieved. More elaborate mouldings – favourite classical ornaments such as egg and dart or clusters of acanthus leaves – are more likely to be carved by craft workers on site, using small fine saws and a range of abrasives.

The state rooms reveal the English taste for classicism tempered with sumptuous decoration. It was the fashion to display paintings against a background of rich velvet and damask wall coverings. These are still preserved in opulent rooms like the saloon, where Rubens's *Return from Egypt* is displayed against a backdrop of red velvet beneath a gilded and coffered ceiling – this time with octagonal panels in the plasterwork. The effect is one of richness – but also control. Discretion, and the guiding hand of classicism, stop the opulence short of running riot.

▲ Kiln at Bulmer Brick and Tile.

Even so, the richness of Holkham and its contents put the Cokes in debt. The Earl was courageous – or reckless – enough to carry on with construction during the twenty-five years it took to complete the building, demanding only the highest quality to the last. In doing so, he showed that Georgian architecture could re-interpret ancient models to produce something thoroughly modern and of its own time. If the house as a whole seemed too vast and opulent to be imitated, elements like the side wings – each of which amounted to a sizeable building in its own right – could be copied. This was one way in which houses on a grand scale could influence the builders of smaller, city dwellings.

A DIVERSITY OF STYLES

Even while Holkham was being built, and influential as it was, English taste was looking in other directions. One was China. Landscape gardeners began to dot their vistas with Chinese bridges, temples, and other fanciful structures. At the heart of this fashion for chinoiserie was Kew Gardens where various structures, including William Chambers's famous pagoda, were erected during the period of Holkham's construction.

Kew also had a 'mosque', built in a hybrid style with Gothic elements that heralded the later fashion for 'Indian' and 'Moorish' buildings which is seen most clearly in S.P. Cockerell's design for the great house at Sezincote, Gloucestershire, topped with an onion dome. But this belongs to the beginning of the nineteenth century, as does the Prince Regent's famous Royal Pavilion at Brighton, a blend of Indian and Chinese styles.

Meanwhile architects were also experimenting with medieval Gothic, adapting it, making it more filigree and fanciful, and rendering vaulting patterns in plasterwork to create an eighteenth-century version of the style, which became known as 'Gothick'. Forms of conventional Gothic had survived, used occasionally in church building since the Reformation. Gothick was a different matter, and was used for country houses such as Horace Walpole's influential house at Strawberry Hill, Twickenham (1747–63). Applied to drawing rooms and dining rooms, which did not exist when Gothic was invented, it looks bizarre and it is understandable that many people regarded it as something totally exotic, a style that could be mixed harmoniously with Chinese design.

If the mid-century saw an explosion of different styles amongst Britain's country houses, classicism had taken hold in the city. The Palladian style was destined to be copied and adapted at lower social levels than had originally been the case. The middle classes were getting richer and aspiring to Holkham's grandeur. The brickwork, sash windows, and elegant details of the great house were soon appearing in small terraced town houses.

THE GEORGIAN TOWN HOUSE

The British brought the Palladian villa into the city and created the Georgian town house. To the casual observer these two building types look rather

◄ Entrance hall, Holkham Hall: alabaster Ionic columns and coffered ceiling.

different, but they have several important features in common. The town house has a similar plan to the villa: a central hall and staircase surrounded by four four-square rooms of identical proportions, two on either side. Within the rooms there are the same beautiful proportions, with balanced, square-headed door and window openings and elegant fireplaces. There are the same well-positioned windows. The elaborations – decorated cornices, fine carving, and similar details – seen in the Palladian villa were 'optional extras' in the town house. Rich residents wanted all these decorative fittings, poorer people made do with the basics. Builders amassed a vocabulary of house plans and details, drawing on the many pattern books that were published in the eighteenth century.

▶ Peckover House, Wisbech, Cambridgeshire, a large town house built in the 1720s.

Pattern books

From the beginning, publishing had a huge impact on the spread of classical architecture in Britain. Isaac Ware, an architect colleague of Burlington, published translations of Palladio's *Four Books* and also produced an edition of Inigo Jones's drawings and a book of engravings of Houghton Hall, Norfolk, which had been designed by Colen Campbell and William Kent. He followed these with *A Complete Body of Architecture* (1756), an encyclopaedia of the Georgian style.

Campbell's *Vitruvius Britannicus* was costly, but in addition to this series there were more popular volumes – pattern books full of examples of architectural elements, house plans, and guides to measurement and proportion. These started to appear in the 1720s and were aimed at the thousands of craftsmen who were putting up houses without the benefit of an architect. The titles often indicate their contents: *The Builder's Chest Book,* or *A Compleat Key to the Five Orders of Columns in Architecture* and *The City and Country Builder's and Workman's Treasury of Designs* are two typical examples. One successful author, Batty Langley, produced a string of clear, well-illustrated books covering everything from measurement and architectural proportions to the classical orders and the best ways to lay out a garden. Books like these were frequently reprinted and were used widely in the building trade for several decades. They were also much copied by the other writers and publishers. As Steven Parissien, architectural historian and author of *The Georgian House*, explains, pattern books were aimed 'not at the great architect, who is presumably properly trained, not at the great patron, who can afford to buy copies of Palladio ... but at the average builder and carpenter'. A pattern book was 'a how-to book, not to teach them their trade, but to show them how to interpret the new Palladian rules and proportions'.

The books provided standard, readily available, kits of features for the Georgian house.Cornices, balustrades, staircases, fireplaces, doorcases, window surrounds – all these and more were presented in a form that a craftworker could easily copy. They also supplied measurements, so that a builder could work out the correct proportions for rooms and their fittings, and even gave instructions on making different types of paint and indications of colours. Above all, they showed the classical orders, and explained them in a way every ordinary builder could understand. Craftsmen learned to think of the parts of an interior wall as relating to the parts of a classical column. The capital at the top of the column corresponded to the cornice running along the top of the wall; the long shaft of the column corresponded to the wall itself; the top of the base aligned with the dado rail; and the plinth matched the skirting boards. It was a simple system to apply and produced well-proportioned, practical walls.

At the same time, burgeoning industry supplied cheaper materials – brick, wood, iron, and glass – which could be transported more easily and cheaply than in the past using the new network of canals. Now British builders also had guides to help them use and arrange these materials in a fashionable way. Not surprisingly, almost identical terraces of houses based on these guidelines began to appear in towns and cities all over Britain.

'THE TRICK WAS TO ARRANGE THE COMPONENTS TO CREATE MODELS TO SUIT ALL CUSTOMERS'

The structure of most Georgian houses was the same, whether their occupants were rich or poor. The windows were ordered neatly across the 5-metre street frontage of a typical middle-class house, with the front door offset to one side. The wooden joists that supported the floor went from the front to the back of the house, supported by a load-bearing wall in the middle. Floorboards were laid across the joists, and therefore ran parallel with the street frontage. There was a pitched roof in two sections, both of which sloped down to a valley in the centre of the house. But because the front wall continued upwards past the servants' floor the roof was concealed from view, giving the house the more 'classical' appearance demanded by builders and clients alike.

The structure was controlled by law. There had first been concern about the quality of house-building after the Great Fire of London in 1666 and the following century or so saw a succession of acts passed by Parliament to regulate building in cities. Perhaps the best of these was the Building Act of 1774, the first that tried to tie builders down to a set code of practice and force them to work within strict parameters. The act defined four different grades or 'rates' of houses and set down basic specifications for each – minimum dimensions for the rooms, what materials the builder should use, the minimum thickness of the brick walls, and so on. 'First rate' houses were the larger homes in the grander speculative developments, aimed at leading professional people like lawyers and doctors. At the other end of the scale were the small 'fourth rate' houses intended for poorer working people.

Most of the houses were laid out in a similar way. At street level were the everyday reception rooms, decorated in quite a plain style. On the first floor, or *piano nobile*, there were the grander reception rooms, with larger windows. The decoration here was more lavish, but still based on pattern books. Above were the family bedrooms. These were also well decorated, though with a lighter touch than the main reception rooms. Higher still were the basic, functional quarters of those servants who did not live in the basement, next to the kitchen. From the outside, a hierarchy of

'THEY TOOK THIS PERFECT MODEL AND ROLLED IT OUT TO CREATE THE WHOLE CITY ON THE SAME PRODUCTION LINE'

window sizes reflected this arrangement, with smaller windows at the top and in the basement, and the largest ones on the *piano nobile*. The way these rooms were used was not as well defined as the layout suggests. Room functions were not as rigid in the eighteenth century as they are today and it was not uncommon for a host to receive guests in his bedroom, or for there to be a bed in a reception room.

The lightness of Georgian rooms is a modern misconception. Large sash windows could make the houses light during the day but at night, lit by a few candles, an eighteenth-century room was much darker than today's electrically lit interiors. Candlelight, flickering and directional, picked out features such as cornices and dado rails, giving dramatic shadows and making the walls seem more three-dimensional than they do under electric light.

Sash windows

One of the greatest inventions of the late seventeenth century is the sliding sash window. No one knows for sure who devised it, but it was probably conceived among the circle of intellectuals and designers who grouped around Christopher Wren. This was a forum of formidable minds who discussed topics as diverse as astronomy and architecture. Wren was certainly one of the first architects to use sash windows, and they became a key component of the houses of the Georgian period.

They succeed because they are simple. The two glass sections move up and down in parallel grooves, counterbalanced by weights concealed in the sides of the frame. The structure can be made with thin timbers that allow large panes of glass to be used. These Enlightenment windows throw a generous light into the room.

Sash windows are efficient ventilators. Pulling up the bottom sash very slightly admits the merest trickle of fresh air in between the two panes before any gap appears at the bottom of the window – and keeps the air changing without causing a draught. Alternatively, opening both sashes so that there are gaps at the top and bottom creates a brisk circulation of air.

Sash window technology did not stand still. Builders developed their use of materials, replacing rope sash cords with metal chains and employing pulleys of brass or iron instead of the woodern pulleys originally fitted. Early 'sash windows did without catches, but fasterners became more common as the eighteenth century progressed.

The appearance of English houses was transformed by these windows. Such large areas of glass had never before been seen in ordinary houses, which also acquired a new vertical emphasis as a result of the tall sashes. Sash windows have never really been bettered and have remained a vital ingredient in the British townscape to this day.

TRANSFORMING THE TOWNS

Because of the need to rebuild after the fire of 1666 and the fact that the population doubled in the following century, London took the lead in creating town houses, and districts like Spitalfields still give an idea of what the new townscape looked like. The streets were ordered and many had pavements for the first time. But there was still much variety with different-sized houses nearby, different street frontage designs – all nonetheless unified because their proportions were similar.

Builders and landowners soon realized that the need for new houses provided them with an opportunity to make money. In spite of the efforts of Christopher Wren, there had been no grand rebuilding plan to reshape

▾ Bedford Square, London, brick-built town houses of 1775–80.

London after the fire. It was up to individual landowners to redevelop their sites. Soon they were creating miniature cities within the city, developments of squares and terraces designed to look attractively grand. Terraces began to look like palaces, with rows of classical columns in the middle and protruding wings at either end. The look of the great country houses was coming to town, and soon thousands of people wanted to live behind impressive facades like these.

Builders were helped by a new material, stucco, which they could apply to walls, columns, and pediments to clothe a building in a covering of uniform creamy brown. It looked good, and the details of mouldings and other ornamentation cut down on the uniformity. But the beauty was only skin-deep, and underneath the facades there were still the same standard terraces. London was starting to become a city of pretend palaces.

'A HUGE SWING IN FASHION MADE THE CITY A COOL PLACE TO LIVE'

A rising population, successful industry, and better transport of materials produced a boom that saw terraced Georgian houses built in their thousands. The faces of many of Britain's towns were transformed, and landowners realized they could make fortunes from housing. They did this by selling leases. The era of speculative building arrived. Builders threw up new terraces as fast as they could and landlords sold ninety-nine-year leases to prospective occupants. Even though construction was rapid, the landlord's investment was large and both builders and their clients often sailed close to the wind. As architectural historian Dan Cruikshank explains: 'They cut corners all the time because the speculators were on the edge of bankruptcy. But they knew which corners to cut and get away with it. These houses built to last sixty or eighty years have lasted two or three hundred. Because they're built of soft materials – soft wood and lime mortar – they can bend with time, and the buffets of bombing and so on, and have this weird extra life.' Some builders, those with the least working capital, put up only the brickwork shell of the structure, plus the roof and floors. The occupiers added everything else – doorcases, mouldings, even panelling. Even these buildings have lasted, and their extra life continues with many such houses converted to offices.

THE SPLENDOURS OF BATH

Many provincial towns were transformed and the new London streets and squares were impressive, but grander than either was the ultimate society town, the centre of fashion from the 1700s onwards: Bath. People had known about its healing waters since before the Roman occupation and these were rediscovered when Queen Anne visited the city in 1702 and 1703. In 1705 the corporation appointed Richard Nash (famous as 'Beau Nash') as 'master of ceremonies', and he was the first to realize that Bath could be made into a place that everyone wanted to see, and where everyone wanted to be seen.

Nash supplied the vision, but the men who transformed this vision into bricks, mortar and stone were the architects John Wood and his son, also called John. In 1728 John Wood the Elder began pushing the city into new territory with Queen Square. It was followed by terraces and the Parades (designed around a sunken garden). His crowning achievement was the

▾ Royal Crescent, Bath.

Circus, a circle of thirty-three houses divided into three eleven-house sections. It is clean-cut, grand, and must have looked modern in 1754 when building began. Yet the Circus respects the traditions of classical design. There is a hierarchy of orders – the simple Doric at the bottom, then Ionic, and finally the elaborate Corinthian at the top.

The Circus leaves no doubt about the values of Nash and Wood. Above all, this is architecture to impress. The houses fit into the grander scheme, masked by rows of columns – of which it seems there can never be too many. Each street fits into a still larger overall scheme of dramatic vistas. Both men knew that people would come to Bath, see these houses, and want to live in them. As Colin and Rose Bell put it in their book *City Fathers*, this was 'building designed to create a need, not answer one'.

John Wood the Elder died in 1754, the year work started on the Circus, and his son took over and created an even more stupendous composition: Royal Crescent. Here the facade is made up of a wall of columns. The sweep of the frontage is vast, and open greenery sets the crescent off to perfection. It is the most famous neo-classical facade in the world, and rightly so.

THE VOGUE FOR THE SPA

Everyone wanted to buy into the style and fashion created by Bath. The city boomed, and others grew to rival it as spas became the fashion. Tunbridge, an established spa in the seventeenth century, expanded rapidly and others such as Scarborough and Leamington developed later in the eighteenth century. Cheltenham, made fashionable when George III visited it in 1788, grew on into the nineteenth century.

Each of these towns has features that derive from Bath: squares and crescents, classical-style houses, facades designed to impress. But there is a falling off in quality. Builders in the nineteenth century turned increasingly to brick, covered with stucco to imitate Bath's stone. The need to build quickly seemed to lead to a coarsening of detail, although there are exceptions – the inventive use of decorative wrought-iron balconies in Cheltenham is an example. However, for grandeur of design realized in stone there is nothing in England to equal Bath.

EDINBURGH

It is a different story in Scotland. Edinburgh was still a medieval city in the early eighteenth century, its narrow, winding streets crammed with tall, crowded tenements. However, it housed a middle class whose members were well educated and increasingly rich. They aspired to something better and in the mid-eighteenth century began to look for ways of improving and extending their city. In 1766 the city council invited architects to submit plans for a 'new town' that would make the city bigger and provide more convenient housing.

The council selected a plan by the twenty-five-year-old James Craig and gave it the go-ahead in 1767. The plan did far more than address Edinburgh's housing

▼ Terraced houses in Edinburgh's New Town.

crisis. It brought ordered town planning and classical architecture from the south; it provided a worthy home for the capital's classically educated élite; it made Edinburgh truly a new 'Athens of the North'.

This was town planning on a grand scale. The basic model is a simple grid, interrupted by a pair of squares, one at either end of a long central avenue. A basic set of rules was laid down – all the buildings were to be aligned, for example, and pavements were to have a standard 10-foot width. Later, after building had begun, the authorities introduced further regulations to unify the scheme. Buildings on the main streets were to have no more than three storeys and dormer windows were not permitted. Although these rules were not always observed, they helped foster a basic unity in the streets of the New Town.

Another unifying feature was the material. Like Bath, Edinburgh was a city of stone. As architectural historian David Walker, puts it, 'We had very little brick in Scotland at that time – we had so much good stone that we didn't need to use it. The result was that everything was very solid and very expensive.' So solid, indeed, that Edinburgh's terraces, built to last, have changed little in the last 300 years. It is not for nothing that the standard Scottish lease, unlike its southern counterpart, was for 999 years.

The expansion of Edinburgh did not stop with Craig's plan. Other landowners – the Earl of Moray, Henry Raeburn, and Francis Walker – followed suit, weaving together terraces and circles, ellipses and crescents, in nearby districts. On the whole, they kept to the New Town style of sober classicism which, with its large scale and good proportions, is impressive even today. Regularly spaced windows were essential to make the proportions work, so if a staircase or chimney on the inside was in the way the builders put in false windows. These could be made of stone and then painted or, for an even more authentic look, real glass windows were installed over black-painted stone. Whichever method was used, a casual observer misses the difference between false and real.

Most New Town houses are large, but scaled-down versions were built for those who could not afford them. Many terraces therefore have corner blocks of flats, but these are cleverly disguised – usually to look like a pair of individual houses – so that the pattern of large-scale units is not broken. This integration helps to give the New Town social variety, making it less a housing estate for the rich and more a place where different classes live side by side.

Details of doorways in the New Town, Edinburgh. From top to bottom these are Corinthian, Ionic and Doric.

ANTIQUITIES OF ATHENS

It was no accident that Edinburgh became the *Athens of the North*. For although the Palladians in the early eighteenth century had looked to the classical architecture of Rome, there was a movement towards the end of the century to study, value, and imitate the ruins of Greece. One of the earliest hints of the fashion for things Greek was when engravings of the ruins of the Greek temples at Paestum, Sicily, were published during the 1750s and 1760s.

Early in the 1750s the architects James Stuart and Nicholas Revett mounted a survey of the remains of ancient Athens. It was exacting work, in conditions that must often have been difficult and dangerous, but after a long gestation the first volume of their *The Antiquities of Athens* was published in 1762. Over the next seventy years, and with the help of several other architect-surveyors, four further volumes appeared. The books, especially the first two volumes, stimulated a love of Greece amongst the British aristocracy, became standard works for a revival of the Greek architectural style, and earned their first-named author the nickname 'Athenian' Stuart.

By the beginning of the nineteenth century British buildings were regularly showing signs of the Greek influence. William Wilkins was one of the first architects to exploit its motifs on a large scale. His country house at Grange Park, Hampshire (1804-9) has a huge Doric portico which takes up one entire facade of the building and looks just like the front of a Greek temple. The style is plain and uncompromising and, looking at the house from the right angle, it is almost as though one of the antiquities of Athens has appeared in the Hampshire countryside. Decimus Burton's London Athenaeum Club (1829–30) and Thomas Hamilton's Edinburgh High School (1825–9) are other major examples of this severe English Doric. The British Museum (1823–46), designed by Robert

Smirke, uses the more slender Ionic order and its rows of columns and carved pediments also speak of Greece, reflecting the world of the Elgin marbles, which had arrived in Britain between 1801 and 1812.

Other Greek revival buildings mix Athenian elements with more humour and eclecticism. One of the most famous monuments of the Greek revival is St Pancras Church, London (1819–22), designed by William and H.W. Inwood. It has a fairly straightforward Ionic portico, apparently based on the Erechtheion, the temple next to the Parthenon on the Acropolis. Above the portico is an extraordinary octagonal steeple which is like a cannibalization of two notable Athenian monuments: the Tower of the Winds and the Choragic Monument of Lysicrates. The architectural historian John Summerson referred to this building's 'innocent ingenuity', an appropriate way to describe the architects' daring raid on 'Athenian' Stuart's engravings and the fragments brought back to Britain by Lord Elgin. To see what virtuosity the Greek style could yield in less innocent hands, one must look at a contemporary housing and town-planning scheme to the west of St Pancras.

JOHN NASH AND REGENT'S PARK

In London, the Georgian terrace becomes the grandest of all city palaces in John Nash's work in Regent's Park. In the early nineteenth century a large tract of crown land that stretched from central London to the present park had become available and in 1811 Nash became both its architect and developer. He was an enthusiast for the Picturesque, borrowing Gothic motifs to build country houses that looked like tamed castles, and adding fanciful towers and verandas to houses in the classical style.

Some of this fancy design influences the terraces, squares, and crescents that Nash laid out around Regent's Park. Although the buildings are

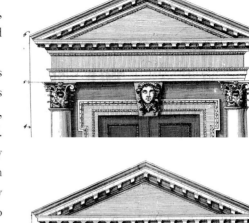

▲ Doorway pediments from the pattern book, *The British Architect*, 1758, showing the Corinthian, Ionic and Doric styles.

nominally in the Greek style, houses everywhere in the area take on the most extraordinary disguises. The typical Georgian terrace, with protruding bays at either end and a colonnade and triangular pediment in the centre, was not enough for Nash. Cumberland Terrace is vaster than any palace; its central feature, a pediment crowned with statuary, is itself the size of a large terrace and is supported by a row of sixteen Ionic columns, each the height of two interior storeys. To each side is a great sweep of houses, punctuated with square bays of a further four columns each. Grand archways give access to the mews behind, and statues and other ornamental details look out over the parapets.

'THE MATERIAL IS STUCCO BUT IT MIGHT AS WELL BE ICING SUGAR'

The Ionic columns and the frieze of statues in the pediment at Cumberland Terrace suggest the Greek origins of this style. But there is no faithfulness to ancient sources, little heed paid to the rules of classicism, not even the unity of Wood's terraces in Bath or Edinburgh's New Town. It is all done for magnificent effect, and the white stucco details bear little relation to either structure or interior.

Around and behind Cumberland Terrace are other Nash terraces, though far fewer than he originally planned. He had intended to build further streets of villas, terraces, and an elaborate double circus, together with barracks for the Horse Guards and a pleasure house for the Prince Regent. The scheme was curtailed, but it is still a monument to his grand concept, still an amazing development in the line that runs from ancient Greece and Rome, through Palladio and Jones to the Georgians, still the most audacious piece of city planning London has seen.

From tiny 'fourth rate' dwellings to gargantuan terraces like those in Regent's Park, the Georgian style proved one of the most adaptable in the history of domestic architecture. Like the products of a modern motor manufacturer, its houses came in a range of standard models to suit every pocket. Each could be customized to the order of the original owner, who could specify features from fireplaces to door surrounds, cornices to skirting boards. Although they were not built to last, these elegant houses have proved some of the most durable, and best loved, of all British buildings.

▶ Cumberland Terrace, Regents Park, London.

MODERN PARALLELS

Classicism has little obvious in common with the Modernist architecture of the twentieth century. Modernist architects saw classicism as a style of the past, as something to rebel against. The orders, with their fancy columns and carved entablatures, were something to reject in a world where form was supposed to follow function.

Of course, classical buildings were built in Britain in the twentieth century. In Quinlan Terry's redevelopment of Richmond Riverside (1988), the architect tries to bring some of the elegance of the Georgian period to a frontage of modern offices and shops. The effect is of several facades jostling together, trying but failing to give the impression that they have been built at different times. Inside, modern offices give the lie to the classical exteriors.

Modern architects have had other, very different, takes on classicism, which can be compared to Modernism in the staggering impact it must have had on contemporaries. But the styles have more than their impact in common. Both are intellectual and austere. And they have many other common features, as revealed in a building like the Royal College of Physicians (1964) by Denys Lasdun. This building has four-square proportions, is set off with a triangulated pediment, has its main rooms on the first floor or *piano nobile*, and is built of a material – concrete – that is mostly white. Its values are intellectual, rational,

▸ The Royal College of Physicians, London, by Denys Lasdun.

and simple, but it has a certain grandeur, like many Palladian buildings. All these attributes make Lasdun's building similar to the classical buildings of earlier times – even the lower floor of brick seems to recall the rusticated bases of Palladian houses. It is like a ghost of the Palladian style.

There are also modern residential buildings that pick up on many of the traits of classicism. London's The Circle, designed by Piers Gough's firm CZWG, is a block of flats with a curving facade that recalls the eighteenth-century crescent or circus and uses repetition in the facade to give an impression of geometrical order, like a Georgian terrace. It is also built of uniform parts, though with materials such as concrete and steel which give fewer constraints than the Georgians' materials imposed. The bright blue of the facade stuns passers-by, but in the eighteenth century people were almost as surprised by the brand-new classical grandeur of Georgian terraces.

▲ The Circle, London, by architects CZWG.

chapter five

The Manic Street Builders

THE VICTORIAN REVOLUTION IN BUILDING

The Victorian period was one of the most exciting in British building. It was an era of great advances in construction, when iron and glass fulfilled their potential as building materials, giving architects and engineers unprecedented new freedoms. There was the freedom to create vast interior spaces, like the Crystal Palace or the train sheds of big railway stations. There was the freedom to burrow into the earth and build the world's first underground railways. And there was the freedom to create new types of building in response to the snowballing growth of trade and industry.

All these freedoms could lead to buildings in which the materials and engineering dictated the appearance of the result. The structure of a Victorian

▸ Piers Gough outside the Midland Grand Hotel, London.

train shed or warehouse is there for all to see, a glorious display of iron, glass, and brick. There was also a contrary movement in Victorian architecture, a realization that the new engineering skills could provide hidden support for structures in virtually any style. Iron brackets could hold up Gothic staircases. Doric columns on warehouse fronts could be made from iron. The Victorians saw that they could use their technological skills to do any building in any style. They could revive the modes of the past – classical, Gothic, and so on – and use them in new ways. This realization opened a Pandora's box of styles, and began a style war that has been with us, in one form or another, ever since.

BUILDING SITES

Nowhere were these developments more obvious than in the capital. Victorian London was constantly changing. At the heart of a world empire, it was growing month by month. At ground level, railways and canals were criss-crossing the city. Between them, buildings shot up with staggering speed – houses, law courts, schools, hotels in the centre of town; warehouses, factories, and more houses further out. The range of materials and styles was unprecedented. The Victorians were insatiable builders and their capital was like one huge building site.

The greatest disruption of all was caused by the building of London's first underground railway lines. The city's roads had become congested as never before. Carts, carriages, horse-drawn omnibuses, pedestrians, horses – all manner of traffic was competing for space. In addition, conditions were filthy. Horse dung and rubbish made some streets unpleasant and even impassable for pedestrians. The best solution was to go below the ground. But a true underground railway system had never been built before. How could it be achieved?

THE FIRST UNDERGROUND RAILWAYS

The earliest underground lines followed the routes of main streets. Engineers removed the road surfaces and opened up enormous trenches. At the bottoms of these, they laid ballast and track, put in signalling, and built all the fixtures and fittings needed for a steam-driven railway of the time. Then they roofed over the

'THESE WEREN'T ELECTRIC, BUT FIRE-BREATHING STEAM TRAINS'

trenches with great arches up to nine bricks in thickness and reinstated the roads above. The method, called cut and cover, was used for inner-city underground railways like the Metropolitan, Northern, and Circle lines. The trains ran along the same routes as the above-ground omnibuses, competed for their passengers, and transformed big-city transport for good.

The Metropolitan Line, which originally ran from Paddington to Farringdon Street, opened to the public in 1863. Passengers could walk down a flight of stairs to another world beneath the streets. They were amazed, and rather frightened, by the idea of a railway running under the ground, a train hurtling along at speed with no view but the black walls of the tunnel. *The Times* reflected public disquiet. People, said the newspaper, would never prefer 'to be driven amid palpable darkness through the foul subsoil of London'. But despite the smoky atmosphere of the first underground platforms and the dark unfamiliar tunnels, the idea caught on. It was preferable, after all, to the crowded, smelly, muddy streets above.

The Victorian platforms of Baker Street station have changed little since it was opened. The great brick arches still support the soil and streets above. The flues, designed to let steam out and light in, are still visible, although now they are tiled and fitted with fluorescent lights to make the platforms brighter. There is still something modern, both functional and elegant, about the platforms.

▲ Victorian underground platforms at Baker Street station.

THE TUBE GOES DEEPER

The coming of electricity revolutionized the underground railways. With no steam to dispose of, trains could go more deeply beneath the ground. And this was just as well. In the wake of London's construction boom the soil immediately beneath the streets was becoming more and more congested with water pipes, gas mains, telegraph cables, and sewers. Soon these would be joined by cables for electricity. It made sense to go deeper. But how?

The Victorian engineers began with the lift shafts. The early trains, just below the surface, had not needed lifts. The new, deep tunnels would need a way to get passengers down to platform level. So shafts were sunk every half a mile along the proposed routes. Each had to be wide enough for a pair of lift cars and sufficiently large to remove all the spoil when tunnel-digging began – and they had to be dug by hand.

Digging the shafts took vast amounts of labour, but when this had been completed and the engineers reached track level they had to display ingenuity as well as brawn. They needed a machine capable of slicing through the ground to create the tunnels. The solution was the Greathead shield. Peter Woods of the London Transport Museum explains how it worked: 'It was nothing more than a large pastry-cutter turned on its side and pushed forward through the clay to create a safe working environment for the engineers.' Hydraulic rams pushed the shield through the clay and the spoil was taken out through the lift shafts.

When a tunnel had been excavated to the correct diameter, the engineers fitted cast-iron lining rings which ran around its entire inner surface. A concrete mix, compensation grout, was pumped through holes in the rings into the space between them and the soil, and the holes were then plugged with waxed rope to prevent water seepage.

The rolling stock fitted these narrow, circular tunnels almost exactly – electric trains do not pose such a ventilation problem as steam engines and can therefore run in narrower tunnels. Such ventilation as was needed was provided by the lifts which shifted air up and down their shafts, and by the movement of air caused by the trains themselves. These narrow tunnels some 50 metres beneath the ground soon became known as 'the tube'.

The tunnels were made wider at stations to accommodate platforms, benches, and other passenger facilities. These pedestrian areas were tiled in the practical, hygienic style that has become the hallmark of London's underground. Multicoloured and multi-

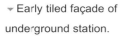
▾ Early tiled façade of underground station.

purpose, the glazed bricks were easy to clean and ideal for the grimy, industrial environment of late nineteenth-century London. Visually, they provided a corporate identity for the railway company. But the visuals did more than this. In Victorian times, there were many people

who could not read or write and the bold, memorable patterns told them where they were, and directed them to the station exit. Different dominant colours for different lines, still used today, enhanced this effect.

The bricks were so successful that they were also used outside. Bold, oxblood-coloured glazed terracotta blocks still cover the walls of many early Northern and Piccadilly Line stations. For the original railway companies they were part of a powerful corporate identity. Londoners today still use them as a way of locating the underground in crowded streets.

STOREHOUSES FOR THE EMPIRE

The explosion of building in London was made possible by Britain's expanding empire and the wealth it brought, and the trading networks that gathered these riches had their own expression in architecture: the docks and warehouses in Britain's major ports. At Liverpool's Albert Dock warehouses that show the modern side of Victoria's empire still survive.

In the Middle Ages, Liverpool had not been a particularly important port. But in 1715 it saw the creation of the world's first commercial enclosed dock. Suddenly, Liverpool was the ideal port with a ready-made and growing industrial hinterland in Lancashire and Yorkshire. Links to the major northern canals ensured that the city could exploit this hinterland and the city burgeoned over the next century. Between 1780 and 1830, it grew forty-fold to become, after London, the country's second biggest port and second largest city.

Liverpool was thriving, but the port had its problems. Smuggling was rife, provoking the customs authorities to crack down on suspect procedures, and this in turn slowed down trade. There was also a spate of fires in warehouses and transit sheds. With new warehouses being built, it was time to make improvements.

The man at the forefront of these was Jesse Hartley, dock surveyor at Liverpool from 1845 to 1860. His monument is the 3-hectare Albert Dock, a warehouse complex of deceptive simplicity. Thousands of tonnes of cargo arrived there every day. Large, secure, fireproof storage spaces were needed for these goods, and Hartley supplied buildings in which engineering tradition and innovation met head-on. Adrian Jarvis, curator of port history at Mersey Maritime Museum, explains: 'One of the marks of a great engineer is that he knows when to innovate and when not to. Innovation is always risky and expensive, so when you look around these buildings, you will find that some parts, like the massive load-bearing brick walls, are perfectly within the comprehension of any competent medieval mason.'

But Hartley modified the medieval mason's approach. Economical brick replaces medieval stone. The walls get thinner as they go up, lightening the load and providing more storage space on the upper floors; and they are reinforced at strategic points with large blocks of hard granite, to protect the soft brick from knocks at vulnerable points such as corners.

The greatest innovations are in the revolutionary roof, a stressed-skin structure that is about 100 years ahead of its time. It is made of 9-millimetre-thick plates of wrought iron, riveted together and bent to form a curve. The curve is the secret of the roof's strength, and tension is the key to keeping it curved. Iron tie rods pull in the whole roof, which does not need support in the middle of the building; it simply rests on the outer walls.

Fireproofing is an important aspect of the building. Innovative shallow brick vaults, supported on wrought-iron Y-beams, are fitted between each floor and if

'A RADICALLY MODERN FACE OF THE EMPIRE'

a fire breaks out their ceilings confine it to the area where it started. The beams rest on pillars but are crudely cast and would have wobbled. So sheet lead was placed between beam and column. If a beam with an uneven base was placed on the lead sheeting, it might press more firmly on one area than another. When this happened, the beam bit into the lead, increasing the bearing surface. As Adrian Jarvis explains, 'It doesn't have to be made perfectly accurately. The best thing to do with precision, if you can, is avoid it, because it costs.'

As dock surveyor, Hartley was also well aware that workers standing idle cost money. Perhaps this is reflected in the design of the lavatory cubicles, which stick out of the sides of the building like the garderobes of a medieval castle. Unpleasant in summer, they would have been unbearably cold in winter, places where no one would want to spend more than the absolute minimum of time.

Hartley's work can be seen in various other places around Liverpool's docks. Stanley Dock (1850–7), for example, survives virtually untouched since 1900 and has been unused since the 1960s. It is battered and uncared for, but with a dignity that still shines through. Here there are more innovations, such as the sliding gate at the dock entrance. When open, the gate slides into a space in one of the piers; when it closes, its edge fits into a groove in the opposite pier. As with the larger warehouses, the massive structure of Stanley Dock seems to express the size and pretensions of the empire, while the details exemplify Victorian inventiveness.

STATION STYLE

Many of Britain's railway companies, who operated lines in different regions, needed a direct link to central London. Each needed a station with a large number of platforms and all the facilities, from ticketing to refreshments, for the thousands of passengers who would be arriving and departing. The problem seemed to demand a new type of building. A series of new railway terminals with vast iron and glass train sheds provided the answer, and the greatest of these was the one at St Pancras, designed for the Midland Railway by engineer W.H. Barlow and opened in 1868.

To Londoners already astounded by train sheds such as King's Cross (1851–2) and Paddington (1852–4), St Pancras was nevertheless still staggering. It held three world records at the time of construction. At around 210 metres, it was the world's longest structure. Its arches covered the world's widest span: 74 metres. And it is still the tallest single-span structure in the world, reaching a height of 32 metres from the railway tracks to the apex of its roof.

This remarkable structure is achieved with a simple form. The span is in the shape of a vast Gothic arch, held together at its base with horizontal steel ties. The ties, however, are invisible, hidden beneath the railway tracks and platforms. The entire structure rests on cast-iron columns and is buttressed by side walls.

▲ St Pancras Station, London: the pointed-arched form of the train shed.

▶ Midland Grand Hotel, London.

This means that the tracks and platforms are in fact above ground level (something that is not apparent from inside the train shed) and a large void is created beneath the tracks. The space was used for storage meeting an important demand at the time. The Burton brewery had asked for somewhere to store the beer they were bringing in to supply London pubs and hotels, so Barlow designed the basement so that the barrels could fit comfortably between the columns.

St Pancras is ruthlessly logical. The entire building – the iron, the glass, and buttress walls – is structure. There is no ornament and everything works. It is like an updating of Gothic, for a modern purpose, but without any of the sculpture that adorns Gothic cathedrals and churches.

If Victorian engineering could be so completely logical it could also be highly illogical, as the building in front of St Pancras station shows. The Midland Grand Hotel is a bizarre conflation of architectural styles, as if the whole empire has converged there in a riot of polychrome brick and marble. One of the most luxurious hotels of its time, its cost amounted to the modern equivalent of £300 million pounds. The hotel is a masterpiece of George Gilbert Scott, one

'GOTHIC STRUCTURE WITH ABSOLUTELY NO FRILLS'

Midland Grand Hotel: interior detail showing Gothic stonework and wall paintings.

of the greatest Victorian architects and an enthusiast of Gothic, and an essay in extravagance. The facade snakes around the corner of Euston and Midland Roads, making the most of its odd-shaped site. Its frontages have rows of Gothic arches with marble shafts and are topped with miniature gables, chimneys, and spires. At one end a clock tower with a spire and pinnacles points to the sky.

Within, the grand public rooms were the height of High Victorian fashion. Most spectacular of all is the main staircase, which rises through three floors. It rests on exposed iron beams but is surrounded with plaster ornament. Ceiling and wall paintings celebrate the eight virtues and the railway company itself whose coat of arms is displayed in lavish colour. Long, skylit corridors lead to some 500 rooms. In the 1870s, the hotel was an ideal place for the middle classes – merchants, businessmen, and their families, coming from the Midlands and the north – to stay on their visits to London. But its heyday was short-lived.

A new generation of hotels, in which elegance and sophistication were valued more than sheer size – the Savoy is an example – was attracting a new generation of Victorians who began to break down barriers between the sexes, allowing women into more of the public spaces that had once been male preserves. The new generation also demanded better sanitary provision. The Midland Grand Hotel did not fit this bill. It had a second life as offices but now stands empty, a monument to the most extravagant of nineteenth-century Gothic styles and to the brief period when the railways prospered.

'A GRAND, CRAZY BIZARRE CONFECTION'

THE GOTHIC REVIVAL

The fanciful style of the Midland Grand Hotel is just one aspect of a wholesale revival of Gothic that took place in the nineteenth century. In many ways this fancifulness is appropriate, since the development had its roots in the Picturesque, a movement that began in the eighteenth century and embraced a love of follies, fantastically ornate cottages and country houses with asymmetrical facades. In the early nineteenth century

castellated buildings gained popularity with some members of the aristocracy, and Scottish baronial style was fashionable in the wake of the novels of Sir Walter Scott. Castellations also appeared on certain structures where massiveness was of the essence – bridge piers and prisons, for example.

As a result, there was a fashion for Gothic details, often treated in a free and easy way, on buildings in the late eighteenth and early nineteenth centuries. The style, usually called 'Gothick', owed little to archaeology or historical authenticity. In the 1830s, however, a few architects began to look more closely at medieval Gothic buildings. The one who looked most closely was A.W.N. Pugin, who published the highly influential *Contrasts* in 1836. Pugin's book compared medieval towns and buildings with the destructive effect of more recent classical and industrial architecture. Gothic was shown to be the better, more morally uplifting, style. In the same year as *Contrasts*, Charles Barry's Gothic design was accepted for the new Houses of Parliament. The style had the backing of the government.

For Pugin, Gothic was the only style. A Catholic convert, he held it almost as an article of faith to build churches in it, to let ritual and sacrament drive his church plans, and to decorate his churches with the most beautiful paintings, sculptures, and glass. In Catholic masterpieces like St Giles's, Cheadle, Lancashire, he set a style of Gothic design that was to influence architects working for the Church of England. It was based on the Decorated style of the fourteenth century, in line with a Victorian belief that this form of Gothic represented the climax of English church building. Where Pugin went, other Victorian architects followed.

For the rest of the nineteenth century, most new British churches were built in the Gothic style. But the architects of these buildings did not follow Pugin slavishly. The Gothic Revival is as varied and eclectic as every other aspect of Victorian architecture. Individuals interpreted it in diverse ways. William Butterfield produced buildings in dazzling polychrome brickwork, like All Saint's in Margaret Street, London, and Keble College, Oxford. The high proportions, multicoloured walls, and use of marble in Butterfield's buildings recall Italian Gothic, and reflect critic John Ruskin's enthusiasm for Italy in important books like *The Stones of Venice*. John Loughborough Pearson employed a quieter mode, looking to re-create a more 'correct' vision of medieval Gothic, often influenced by French prototypes. Elegant vaulting, restrained polychromy, and fine spires are his hallmarks. William Burges had a bolder, more massive style that drew heavily on early Gothic; he shared with medieval masons a love of sculpture, from corbels to gargoyles. G.F. Bodley was a great decorator who insisted on close involvement with every aspect of his buildings, especially their wall paintings and stained glass.

There were, then, as many Gothic Revival styles as there were architects. This richness of Gothic, demonstrated in the Middle Ages, was again revealed in the High Victorian period. To architects like Scott, with rich patrons and eclectic tastes, it was a gold mine; and Scott was soon to make it glitter.

GOTHIC OR CLASSICAL?

In 1861 Albert, beloved consort of Queen Victoria, died. A competition was launched for a design for a memorial and George Gilbert Scott won the first prize. Construction began in 1863 and ended in 1872, although the bronze statue of the prince was not fitted until 1876.

'AN ELABORATE JUKEBOX OF A BUILDING'

Like Scott's Midland Grand Hotel, the Albert Memorial is another exercise in fantastic Gothic, a far cry from the careful homages to medieval building that architects such as Pugin, Pearson, or Bodley were designing. Instead of looking to the buildings of the Middle Ages, Scott seems to have taken his cue from medieval metalwork, the caskets and jewellery commissioned by churchmen and aristocrats to house saintly relics and adorn noble bodies.

The Albert Memorial shines. White marble statuary stands out from the plinth. Glass mosaics glitter on the canopy. Details picked out with gilding reflect the sunlight. Coloured stones frame the composition. The whole structure is a jewelled tribute to Albert's interest in craftsmanship and architecture, one that is fitting and that magnifies the style of Gothic metalwork. If Gothic was the style of English patriotism, this is its most intense expression.

Across the road is the prince's other monument: the Albert Hall. In contrast to the memorial, this is built in the classical style. The Victorians were drawn to this style because they thought of themselves as similar to the Romans. They had built up a huge empire; they were innovators and engineers; they could build anything. So the Albert Hall is like a covered version of the Colosseum in Rome or the elliptical Roman amphitheatres of southern France.

The neoclassical style of the Albert Hall is evident in the round- and square-headed openings and classical pilasters, like shallow false columns, that run all around the building. Above these details is a terracotta frieze by Minton, which celebrates the arts, sciences, and industry and relieves this otherwise severe structure which was designed by an engineer, Francis Fowke. The frieze gives the clue to the hall's original name – the Hall of Arts and Science – which appeared on the original plans but was changed when Victoria laid the foundation stone in 1868.

The contrast between the hall and the memorial sums up Victorian architecture. The Gothic and classical styles were often seen as opposites. Classical was south European, Catholic, worldly and reliable; Gothic was north European, Protestant, independent and mystical. The Victorians sometimes argued that the styles were suited to specific building types – Gothic for churches, for example, and classical for public buildings. Although many architects specialized in one style or another this was rarely cut and dried. They were often adaptable, using what they thought best for the circumstances – or following the preferences of the client in a competitive market. So it was that an organization like the Adelphi

▲ Albert Memorial, London.

▲ Albert Hall, London.

Bank could choose an exotic style for their building in Liverpool, while other banks, like the branch of the Bank of England in the same city, could be designed in the classical style.

THE HOUSES OF PARLIAMENT

One of the greatest Victorian buildings, the Houses of Parliament was a prominent example of choosing a style to suit the symbolism of a structure. After the old Palace of Westminster was destroyed by fire in 1834 a competition was announced for a new design, with rules stipulating the style. Gothic and Elizabethan (as in prodigy houses), which were seen as the most specifically British, were the only alternatives.

The winning entry came from Charles Barry, who chose a version of late, Perpendicular Gothic for this national emblem of a building. Working with Barry was Pugin, the most confirmed Gothicist of all, who was responsible for many of the details. Vertical, repetitive, and ornate, the Houses of Parliament seems to suggest that Barry, too, was a confirmed Gothicist. The massive Victoria Tower is an assured piece of Gothic, looking like the great medieval cathedral tower London never had. The smaller Clock Tower, housing Big Ben, has become a symbol of politics and the nation.

Yet Barry was normally more at home with the classical style. He designed, for example, the scholarly, neoclassical Reform Club (1837–41), which draws on both Palladianism and the Renaissance palaces of Florence and Rome. Only the stone gargoyles add a hint of frivolity. Many writers have seen a classical skeleton beneath the Gothic skin of the Houses of Parliament. The river facade, with its repetitions, has a classical symmetry and Pugin accused it of being 'all Grecian'. This is far from accurate, but there is a grain of truth in his overstatement. There is also something classical about the building's plan, with the two chambers ranged on either side of a symmetrical arrangement of corridors and lobbies. In the Houses of Parliament, Gothic and classical elements come together to create a unique blend.

TRANSFORMING MANCHESTER

Like Liverpool, Manchester was one of the north of England's most prosperous cities during the Victorian period. But it did not actually become a city until 1853, and when it did much of the new civic development was in the Gothic style. Perhaps this represented a deliberate decision to take a different path from the great port on the Mersey. Another factor was the presence in the city of a great local architect who became a master of Gothic: Alfred Waterhouse.

In 1863, the council made three decisions that would transform the city centre: first, to create a large formal square there; second, to erect a monument to Prince Albert in the centre of that square; and third, to build a new town hall fronting one side of the square on a difficult, triangular site called the Town Yard. When a competition was announced for a design for the hall, it was natural that Waterhouse should enter. He had already designed important buildings in the city, including the Assize Courts (1859) and the Royal Assurance Building (1861), and he entered an ambitious Gothic plan.

'APPLIED CATHEDRAL EXTERIORS TO A MULTISTOREY OFFICE BLOCK'

The judges decided to assess all the plans according to their performance in a number of different categories and the entries were ranked according to architectural merit, cost, heating, lighting, ventilation, and so on. Waterhouse came only fourth on architectural merit, but top in every other category. He had proved his ability to plan and organize a major public building, so he got the job.

His vast building fulfilled its promise in a mere nine years of construction. Like most of central Manchester's Victorian buildings, it fills the site completely, the facades coming right up to the pavement. These show a confident use of a cathedral Gothic style applied to a secular structure. They also show Waterhouse having fun with the shape of the building. Most of his rivals were baffled by the odd triangular site and placed turrets at the corners to hide the acute angles. But Waterhouse took advantage of the building's strange shape. All along the facades he varied the pace with projecting gables, bays, and turrets. He also played variations on the window sizes, keeping the facades lively, and keeping the viewer's eye moving along them. The building does not have the grace of medieval cathedral Gothic, but it has an ingenuity of its own.

There is still greater inventiveness beneath the building's surface. This lies not so much in the planning – long corridors of offices surrounding a rather claustrophobic central hall with a spiral staircase at each of the three corners – as in the services. The heating is a good example, as Warren Marshall explains: 'In the basements of the stairwells are a series of heat exchangers, and these allowed heat to rise up the building and to be dissipated at each level as the staircases open out.' The long corridors were also heated, the heating pipes concealed by an ornamental metal grille.

Ingenuity also touches the gas supply for the lighting. Beneath the stair handrails is what looks like a metal bar but is in fact a pipe which took gas to the gasoliers that lit the building's public spaces. The Victorians liked multi-purpose features like this. In the same way, they appreciated the

▲ Mosaic flooring at Manchester Town Hall, showing the repeated bee motif.

▶ Manchester Town Hall: the Albert Square façade.

colourful vaulting of the building's long corridors, safe in the knowledge that it was also fireproof.

The Victorians were lovers of symbolism too. Manchester's wealth was founded on cotton and references to this source of prosperity are made throughout the building's decoration. Cotton buds, flowers, and leaves appear in stained glass, wall paintings, and carvings. In some areas they are also linked to imagery of the bee, the emblem of industry and hard work.

ST GEORGE'S HALL, LIVERPOOL

Liverpool's civic centre, by contrast, was created in the classical style. This group of buildings is dominated by St George's Hall, a neo-Greek temple containing a great hall, two courts, and a concert room. This large and confident building was designed by the young architect Harvey Lonsdale Elmes, a Londoner who was only twenty-five when he entered the competition for the job in 1840 and who died of consumption in 1847, long before the project was completed.

It says a lot for the confidence of the people of Liverpool that they chose such a young man to design the hall; it says much for Elmes's own nerve that he designed it in such an uncompromising neoclassical style, even though he had

▸ St George's Hall, Liverpool.

never visited Greece or Rome. But both Elmes and C.R. Cockerell, the architect who took over after Elmes's death and saw the work to completion, had studied their ancient Greek and Roman architecture. They took elements of ancient buildings and reinvented them. So one end of the hall has a standard columned portico with a triangular pediment, a large version of the sort of entrance seen on neoclassical buildings everywhere. But the treatment of the long sides, with rows of columns and a projecting attic storey hiding the roof, is unique. St George's Hall has the mix of tradition and innovation that is the mark of so many successful Victorian public buildings.

The most impressive interior space is the central great hall, with its rows of round arches and curving barrel vault. When they first saw the designs people feared that the weight of the enormous vault would bring the building down, but the engineers came up with a simple yet ingenious way of reducing the weight. They drilled holes in the bricks. This not only lightened the load of the vault but provided a new ventilation system, with foul air escaping through the holes to the outside. And all this is concealed beneath an extravaganza of plaster above marble columns, classical statues, and an ornate tiled floor. It was as if the Victorians could build anything they liked, and did.

▾ A rare façade on which iron columns are exposed between large windows.

IRON FRAMES

St George's Hall, impressive as it was, was a recognizable classical structure. Yet more innovative were Victorian iron-framed buildings. By the time Victoria came to the throne Britain already had a history of using iron for construction. Staffordshire ironmaster John Wilkinson (1728–1808), 'iron-mad Wilkinson', had insisted that you could make anything out of the metal, and even ordered an iron coffin for himself. The world's first iron bridge, at Coalbrookdale, Shropshire, had been built in 1779. By the 1790s, mill buildings (for example at Belper, Derbyshire)

Wrought iron and cast iron

Usable iron was produced in the eighteenth century by mixing the iron ore with charcoal and firing it in a blast furnace. The 'blast' came from powerful bellows (driven by water and later by steam) and brought the mixture to the right heat. The iron absorbed carbon from the charcoal and this reduced the metal's melting point so that it liquefied and collected in the bottom of the furnace. When this smelting process had been completed the molten iron was poured from the furnace and set into pieces called 'pigs'. As these contained various impurities which made the material very brittle, the iron-worker reheated the pigs in another furnace, allowing some of the carbon in the iron to combine with oxygen, reducing the impurities and making the iron stronger and more malleable. This iron could then be hammered into usable shapes

(wrought iron) or poured into moulds to make individual items (cast iron).

During the late eighteenth and nineteenth centuries, ironmasters introduced various improvements in the smelting and reheating process, so that iron became both stronger and more easy to produce in quantity. For example, coke replaced charcoal. This allowed bigger furnaces than before because more iron ore could be piled on to coke than on to charcoal, which tended to crush.

Another improvement was introduced by British inventor Henry Cort, who developed a process called puddling in which the pig iron was reheated in the presence of iron oxide which was stirred into the furnace. Puddling was an effective way of removing impurities to make improved wrought iron.

were being built with cast-iron columns. Some builders had also taken iron into the structure of more conventional buildings, fabricating load-bearing iron beams and columns. In 1796–7, for example, a spinning mill had been built at Shrewsbury with both beams and columns of iron.

Victorian factory owners were quick to see the benefits of a building in which much of the weight was taken by an iron framework. The system did not use up large parts of the floor area, multiple storeys were possible, and the building could be made of standard-size units that could be reproduced with ease and repeated at will to make larger floors. A lower fire risk compared to that in timber-framed buildings was another advantage.

This new type of construction therefore spread with the new building types of the nineteenth century: large factories, warehouses and office buildings. However, perhaps surprisingly, Britain did not embrace all-iron construction. Most buildings concealed their iron frameworks behind brick elevations unlike, say, the iron-fronted buildings of some nineteenth-century American cities.

One man who was more eager than most to celebrate and expose the iron frame was the Liverpool architect Peter Ellis. His Oriel Chambers (1864) barely conceals its industrial structure. Rows of bay windows are lined up between the slimmest stone shafts. To be sure, these conceal the iron framework, but they express it too, suggesting the iron members behind them. The bay windows also use iron, for the narrow glazing bars. These set off large sheets of glass and, if the Gothic pinnacles and ornate gable at the top of the building are ignored for the moment, Oriel Chambers is nearly as close to the 1960s as it is to the 1860s.

This blatant lack of style caused an uproar at the time, as did Ellis's other notable Liverpool building: his high-rise block at No. 16 Cook Street (1866). At the front, the iron frame is once more hidden beneath stone. But elsewhere iron is on display, twisting, for example, with the spiral staircase. At the back of the building, glass stretches across the elevation and the cast-iron structural columns can be clearly seen behind the windows.

At a stroke Ellis had invented modern office-block construction, with metal columns and a 'curtain wall' of glass, some seventy years ahead of its

▲ Oriel Chambers (top) and 16, Cork Street, Liverpool.

time. Neither press nor public was prepared for this sort of construction, this lack of style as contemporaries understood it. There was an outcry, and Ellis turned his back on his city and never worked there again. His revolutionary structures had little influence on other architects – yet glass-and-metal construction had its finest hour in these most Victorian of buildings.

THE GLASSHOUSES

The Victorians collected everything that interested them in the four corners of their empire, from shields and shrunken heads to paintings and plants. The Royal Botanical Gardens at Kew was one beneficiary of plant collecting and in 1839 building began on new houses for the exotic speciments that were arriving from around the world. The first of these was the Palm House, still one of the world's most stunning greenhouses.

A beautiful building, elegant in its simplicity, it is a long structure with a vast central space and a pair of protruding wings. Practically all the main surfaces are curved, creating an effect that has been compared to a large bubble of glass. The

▾ Palm House, Royal Botanical Gardens, Kew.

interior balustrade is cast iron but the main spans, which cover large distances, are wrought iron. This thin material, made possible by heavy Victorian engineering, makes large dimensions possible – the Palm House is 100 metres long, 20 metres wide, and 30 metres high. Wrought iron is also used for some of the finer work , for example the thin ribs that hold the panes of glass in place. There are altogether some 15 miles of wrought-iron ribs and a ingenious system was used to brace them and make the building's skeleton rigid: the builders ran wrought-iron tie rods through cast-iron tubes in a way that allowed them to tighten the rods after assembling the ribs.

About 16,000 panes of glass make up the 'skin' of the Palm House. Today, they are modern plate glass, but in the nineteenth century they were made of a rippling crown glass that gave the structure an even more ethereal, shimmering quality than it has now. However, crown glass, with its rounded bulges, was not ideal for the early inhabitants of the greenhouse.

Iron components

At the beginning of the nineteenth century cast-iron beams and columns became common in mills and factories, where they were valued because they were easy to produce in quantity and were fireproof. Theorists like the mathematician Eaton Hodgkinson worked out the best shapes for cast-iron components, so that beams that combined strength with the minimum of material could be produced, saving both iron and weight. Meanwhile, the repertoire of smaller cast-iron building components was growing rapidly: railings, brackets, verandas, window frames, and many other items were widely available by the beginning of the Victorian period. Many of these components were highly decorative castings, which could be used instead of hand-carved work in wood or stone. Rolling mills were being increasingly used to make structural components in wrought iron (which is stronger than cast iron). Engineer Robert Stephenson used rolled wrought-iron beams in the roof of London's Euston station (1835–9), after which they became more and more common. Improved rolling mills made bigger and bigger beams, as well as the production the strong I-section beam, possible. I-beams made of one piece of rolled wrought iron were first produced in France in 1848.

Wrought iron and cast iron were often used in the same structure, frequently in combination with timber. Standard designs were produced for elements such as roof trusses, and engineers and architects could reproduce these in a range of similar-sized buildings. Larger buildings, from Paxton's greenhouses to the big railway stations, needed special designs to address the challenge of their large spans.

▲ Interior detail, Palm House, Kew, showing iron flowers covering bolts.

It could magnify the sun's rays and many plants shrivelled in the heat. The authorities at Kew ordered it to be changed to a material with a greenish, coppery tinge.

The Palm House was built by the architect Decimus Burton and the engineer Richard Turner, a Dublin man who had designed both boats and greenhouses. Broadly speaking, Burton was the stylist and Turner was responsible for the structure, but the relationship was more complex than this. Burton's first design was criticized for the number of columns it used and, as a result of this criticism, Turner was employed and produced an alternative. Burton in turn attacked this for its Gothic style, saying the building ought to be classical. He then revised Turner's plans, which Turner executed, drawing on Burton's advice about details. So it was that, in a building that seems to wear its structure of iron and glass on its sleeve, some of the details of construction were hidden by decoration. The industrial bolts that hold together many of the iron members are concealed behind elegant iron flowers.

So the style wars that enlivened architectural debates in the nineteenth century even affected accommodation for plants. The result is a building that is neither Gothic nor classical but which, just like the great train sheds of the London railway termini, seems perfectly fitting for its function. But architects were not ready for the next adventure in iron and glass: the hall for the Great Exhibition of 1851.

THE CRYSTAL PALACE

The idea of the Great Exhibition of 1851 sprang from the annual exhibitions held by the Society of Arts and gained a rapid and heady momentum. A group of the great and the good led by the influential designer and civil servant Henry Cole decided to hold an event on a much larger scale than the society's exhibitions, to celebrate the arts and industries of the empire. They approached Prince Albert who was enthusiastic about the idea and agreed to be the exhibition's patron. A royal commission was formed, and its members comprised some of the most

prominent Britons of the time – including politicians of the calibre of Peel and Gladstone. The commission spawned a building committee, which included architects Barry, Cockerell, and T.L. Donaldson and two of the greatest engineers of the time: Robert Stephenson and Isambard Kingdom Brunel. The committee announced a competition to design an exhibition building, and then rejected all

▲ Reconstruction of the exterior of the Crystal Palace, London .

Logistics and mass production

The real innovation behind the Crystal Palace was in the process of producing the components, delivering them to the site, and putting them together. The exhibition hall was not built. It was assembled. And the various parts were manufactured in different places all over the country. Cast-iron columns came from two companies in Dudley, in the West Midlands. The wrought-iron beams for the nave were made in Birmingham in the factory of contractors Fox and Henderson, who also produced wooden components at their mill in Chelsea. Chance Brothers of Birmingham made the glass.

All these components were brought by train directly to the site of the exhibition. They arrived more or less ready for use and at the right time and were taken straight to the place where they were needed.

There was very little stockpiling. There was also very little waste. A few panes of glass were broken, but not much else.

This efficiency meant that the building could be erected at great speed. The entire process, from Paxton's initial design to completion at the Hyde Park site, took less than nine months, and this to cover a space roughly the same size as London's Millennium Dome. The feat is rarely matched, even today.

The Victorians knew this was something extraordinary. As John McKean says, 'Everyone came to see it being built.' The Crystal Palace was constructed to house an exhibition of arts and industry, but the art and industry displayed during its erection was a spectacle in itself.

the entrants. Next they embarked on their own design, but this also floundered and time was running out.

At this point Joseph Paxton came on to the scene. He offered a solution to the problem: a huge iron-and-glass exhibition hall that could be quickly prefabricated and assembled. The speed with which he worked on his idea is legendary. He is said to have done the original rough sketch for what became known as the Crystal Palace on a blotter, during a meeting of the directors of the Midland Railway, and to have worked it up to produce a proper set of drawings over the following eight days, in June 1850. By 6 July the drawings were published in *The Illustrated London News*. Just over a week later, Paxton's design was formally accepted by the committee. The race to construct the building was on.

Paxton's lightning speed, although impressive, was in some ways an illusion. He was using the knowledge of an engineering lifetime, gained working on railway buildings and large greenhouses. He simply adapted this technology to suit a new function and produce a legendary building.

The architectural establishment was uncertain about this revolutionary exhibition hall. As the architectural historian John McKean puts it: 'It annoyed [architects] and I think it frightened them. It was something completely different. In its origination it had no relationship with the world of architecture. In its manufacture it had no relationship with architecture. It was not built by builders, it was built by engineering contractors who had a completely different sort of process. And everyone loved it. I think that's what annoyed the architects most.'

The very inspiration for the Crystal Palace came from outside architecture. Victorian

▲ Reconstruction of the interior of the Crystal Palace, London.

'THE GREATEST REVOLUTION IN BUILDING CONSTRUCTION'

botanists had discovered that people could stand on the leaves of giant water lilies and this gave Paxton the idea for a structure based on very fine structural lines infilled with sheets of wafer-thin material – 'leaves' of glass and 'veins' consisting of wrought-iron glazing bars.

These notions had informed Paxton's earlier designs for greenhouses and conservatories, including a lily house and a large greenhouse called the 'great stove', for the Duke of Devonshire's country mansion at Chatsworth, Derbyshire. In Hyde Park, site of the Great Exhibition, Paxton used his experience of greenhouses to angle the glass carefully so that condensation did not drip on visitors. He rested the glazing bars on wooden beams (the structure was not all iron and glass), and these had an additional purpose. They bore gutters which collected both condensation from within and rain water from outside. Waste water disappeared down the hollow cast-iron columns – another example of dual-purpose Victorian engineering.

The Crystal Palace amazed the Victorians – so much so that they were at first a little frightened of it. Never before had glass been used on such a vast scale, covering a floor area 563 by 124 metres, and some early visitors feared that panes might fall crashing down on their heads. When Victoria arrived to open the exhibition there was concern that the twenty-one-gun salute that greeted her might bring the whole lot down. But the building survived and was a triumph, its three floors displaying the arts and crafts of the empire and entrancing most of its visitors.

After the Great Exhibition closed, Paxton's great palace of glass was taken down and moved to Sydenham, where it remained until it was destroyed by fire in 1936. Many other Victorian buildings, just as revolutionary in design, survive today. The train sheds at the main London railway termini, for example, are still used for their original purpose. Millions of commuters and travellers pass through them every week. We still travel on the underground network, large parts of which were built by the Victorians. Many of our schools, hospitals, factories, and houses are nineteenth-century creations still used in the ways their Victorian builders intended. Yet more factories and warehouses have gained new lives converted to apartments and offices, their structures largely intact. It has become fashionable to sneer at 'Victorian values', but we would be lost without the Victorians' legacy of architecture and engineering. They built the foundations of our world.

MODERN PARALLELS

The Victorians, with their mania for construction, their adoption of new types of building, and their vast stylistic range, probably created more sheer variety of architecture than any preceding people. It is difficult, therefore, to choose the typical Victorian style, let alone the typical Victorian building. Perhaps the Victorians were at their best and most typical in buildings such as their major railway stations, where they used materials like iron and glass in new ways to produce new kinds of architectural space.

We are still capable of producing the impact of Victorian train sheds when we build new stations today. The tube station designed by Norman Foster for Canary Wharf combines grandeur with user-friendliness. A domed glass entrance hall provides plenty of light. The huge ticket hall, massively simple at 280 metres long and 24 metres deep, is big but not disorienting. Like his Victorian predecessors, Foster has used modern materials – in his case, steel, glass, and concrete – to create a working building in a celebratory style.

One of the most important links between Victorian structures like St Pancras or Crystal Palace and modern buildings like Canary Wharf station is the use of glass. Ever since load-bearing steel frames made skyscrapers possible, this has become the favourite material of modern architecture. If the frame takes a building's weight, the walls do not have to bear a heavy load and so modern skyscrapers are often clad in a 'curtain wall' of glass. Today, city buildings can be faced almost entirely with glass, giving residents and office workers plenty of natural light while modern heating and ventilation systems take care of warming and cooling.

Modern glass-clad buildings like James Stirling and James Gowan's Leicester University Engineering Building (1959–63) and Barry Gasson's gallery for the Burrell Collection, Glasgow (1983) are distinguished structures, in which the use of glass

▾ Canary Wharf station, by Norman Foster.

▲ A modern train shed: Nicholas Grimshaw's Waterloo International Terminal.

is handled with care and flair. In the Leicester building, Stirling and Gowan used glass like polythene, to 'wrap' the different spaces and rooms so that they can be whatever size and shape is required. Lecture rooms can be wedge shaped, a spiral staircase can be enclosed in a cylinder of glass, workshops can be lit from above. In the case of the Burrell Collection, the glazed spaces recall Victorian conservatories, the windows drawing the eye to the trees outside the building, and back to the exhibits – and the tree-like concrete columns – within.

These two buildings, then, use glass in very different ways, both of which reflect the artful use of the material pioneered by the Victorians. But modern glass can have a range of qualities unknown in the nineteenth century. Whereas builders then had to put up with glass that was brittle, thin, and difficult to handle, the modern material can be laminated, thick, tough – and even bullet-proof. The versatility of glass is so great that we tend to take it for granted.

Every so often, though, a building comes along that still manages to shock us with new uses for glass. Appropriately, the National Glass Centre at Sunderland, opened in 1998, is just such a building. The entire structure, both walls and roofs, is made of glass – some 3,250 square metres of it. Most striking of all is the large, flat glass roof, made of sheets 1.5 metres square and so tough that they can easily support a man standing in the middle. Buildings like this are proof that architects can still use glass as creatively and inventively as the Victorians.

'NATIONAL GLASS CENTRE – YOU CAN SEE EVERYONE, EVERYWHERE, AND THEY CAN SEE YOU'

▾ National Glass Centre, Sunderland, by Andy Gollifer.

chapter six

The White Stuff

THE MANY STYLES OF MODERN ARCHITECTURE

When we think of twentieth-century architecture, we think of rapid change, of a diversity of styles, of an abundance of new building technologies. All of the century's many scientific, technological, and social changes brought with them the demand for new types of buildings – laboratories, airport terminals, cinemas, leisure centres, petrol stations – and new varieties of every existing type, from houses to factories. Additionally, there were new takes on the city and its planning and fresh looks at alternatives to inner-city life. Architects and engineers came together to meet these demands in varied and exciting ways and as they did so made buildings metamorphose beyond belief. The twentieth century was not only the century of high-rise, but also saw the development of underground bunkers and subterranean 'earth-sheltered' houses. Above all, a rich palette of materials enabled architects to create anew. The twentieth century was the century of steel, glass, and, supremely, concrete, the 'white stuff' that enabled architects to build, sculpt, and mould their creations as never before.

Buildings of steel and concrete could be large, strident, and shocking. Ironically, however, the beginnings of modern architecture are much quieter and more subtle. They can be traced, not to city centres with tall office blocks, but to the suburbs where the British, at the start of the twentieth century, created a way of life that was imitated all over the world.

Suburban living seems traditional now, but early in the century it was a relatively new idea. Hitherto, people had mostly lived and worked in the same district. For most men and women, the main form of transport was by foot. Suddenly, with the arrival of the suburbs and new transport links,

▾ Piers Gough at the de la Warr Pavilion.

people could live at the very edge of London and travel to work in the city on the train or underground. The suburbs also benefited from being near to the country, and their leafy streets and cottage-like houses reflect this.

THE GARDEN SUBURB

The most influential of all the early suburbs was Hampstead Garden Suburb, established in 1907 to address the twin ills of inner-city slums and poor country housing. It was made possible by the extension of the tube line northwards to Golders Green and by a charitable trust set up by Mrs (later Dame) Henrietta Barnett to buy more than 300 acres of land nearby. Some 80 acres was set aside for an extension of Hampstead Heath; the remainder formed the site of the suburb itself, planned by Raymond Unwin and Barry Parker, designers of another influential development: the recent Letchworth Garden City.

The idea was to provide houses for all classes of people. There were flats for the workers, detached houses for the middle classes, and still larger houses for the wealthy. There was even special housing for single people. M.H. Baillie Scott's Waterlow Court, for example, was originally meant to contain flats for single working women. Henrietta Barnett's hope was to benefit the lower classes by allowing them to live near those who were better off, making good housing and a pleasant environment available to all. The environment was made yet more pleasant by keeping the density of houses relatively low, by using hedges as property boundaries, and by letting some of the streets curve in an attractively rustic way.

▲ Flats at Hampstead Garden Suburb, London.

The housing itself has a distinctive style: the backward-looking, almost medieval manner of the Arts and Crafts Movement which had been founded by a group of craftworkers who were followers of the nineteenth-century designer, poet, and socialist William Morris. They believed in the importance of craftsmanship and its application to everything we use, from furniture and buildings to jewellery and textiles. They

'A THIRD WAY, CONTAINING THE BEST OF URBAN AND COUNTRY LIFE' wanted ordinary, everyday objects to be well designed and handmade, in the tradition of the medieval artisans whose work they so much admired.

From an architectural point of view, they therefore admired the traditional vernacular style of timber-framed medieval and Tudor houses. And timber framing is evident all over Hampstead Garden Suburb. Along with this went the doctrine of truth to materials. In other words, materials should be on display, doing the job that they seem to do. In a house by Baillie Scott, for example, the timber frame, visible from the outside, is holding up the building just as it would have done a medieval hall or Tudor house. This would become an ideal embraced by later architects of a much more Modernist stamp.

SIR EDWIN LUTYENS

The planners of Hampstead Garden Suburb wanted a centrepiece that stood out from the rest of the development and called on Sir Edwin Lutyens, the most versatile of Edwardian architects, who could handle a variety of styles with a wit and confidence all his own. At the heart of the suburb, Lutyens laid out two squares, each with a church and other public buildings. The most notable element in this complex is St Jude's church. Its strong shapes and lines, achieved by means of raids on several different styles of the past, mark the building out. The great roof, sweeping almost to the ground and pierced with dormer windows, shows the vernacular influence. The tower and spire have called to mind styles as diverse as Norman, Tudor, and Byzantine. Inside, a Renaissance-style barrel vault in the nave clashes with open timber roofs of bizarre originality over the side aisles. The whole, especially the striking exterior, shows Lutyens's skill in handling a diversity of styles.

He did this best of all in his country houses. Here, there is plenty of evidence of the influence of medieval vernacular. But everywhere it is tempered with discreetly modern features that give hints of the architecture to come. In addition, there is Lutyens's special ingredient: a quirky humour that seems to make his work still more relevant to today.

Deanery Gardens, Berkshire (1901) is one of his finest houses. Traditional materials – stone and brick – are very much in evidence and Lutyens makes clever play with them, using the contrast between red brick

▲ Deanery Gardens, Sonning, Berkshire, by Edwin Lutyens.

and white stone to make beautiful geometrical patterns. The cross-cut vault over the entrance is an example. There is further geometrical play in the courtyard, where a square space is the frame for a circular pool and octagonal patterns in the paving.

Standing back from the facade, it is possible to appreciate how Deanery Gardens typifies the Arts and Crafts style, taking as it does elements of the vernacular house and exemplifying them. The big roof, the horizontal strings of windows, the timber supports and jettied storey, the tall chimney stacks – all these features are exaggerations of the vernacular. But they are exaggerations with a touch of wit. For example, the long windows come together at a corner – but this glazed corner has no upright support, something a medieval builder would never have omitted. In this outwardly traditional-looking house, Lutyens delighted in breaking the rules.

The massive buttresses against the outer wall work in a similar way. Structurally, they were probably not necessary; they are there mainly for show, as a vernacular detail. Looking closely, however, one can see how lovingly this detail has been created. The bricks that make up each sloping buttress have been laid with a gentle upward curve, so that

'TAKES THE MEDIEVAL HOUSE AND MAKES IT MORE EXQUISITELY ITSELF' they start at right angles to the wall and finish at right angles to the slope. Every detail counts in Lutyens's play with surfaces and materials.

Inside, the creativity with forms and details continues. There is a similar patterning of brick and stone. There are barrel vaults to the ceilings. There is a long gallery, like an Elizabethan room with a stunning oak frame, although this acts not as a place for exercise as it would have done in Tudor times but as an elaborate corridor to the many guest bedrooms. Most striking of all is the house's largest room, not a drawing room but a high great hall. Clearly this is a space in which modern comforts are important. Few medieval halls had such vast, floor-to-ceiling windows as the one here which givies a view on to the garden. But there is still an oak frame, wrought at the end into curving patterns, which alludes to the room's medieval inspiration. The fact that it is on display, in the most important room of the house, points once more to the Arts and Crafts doctrine of truth to materials.

SUBURBAN OR MODERN?

The country houses of Edwin Lutyens are in many ways a far cry from the socialist ideal of the garden suburb. Instead of a pleasant environment that can be enjoyed by all classes, buildings like Deanery Gardens were big houses for rich clients. Yet both types of architecture, united by truth to materials, had a wide currency. In Britain, the garden suburb and garden city movement had a strong influence on the new wave of local authority housing. The Watling Estate, Hendon (begun in 1926) was planned as a garden suburb for the less well off. The houses were finished in red brick, roughcast render, or weatherboarding, and these finishes and the estate's curving streets, owed something to Hampstead and similar schemes.

As time went on, the influence spread to suburbs everywhere, although it was often the style rather than the substance of Arts and Crafts that was imitated. Street after street of mock-Tudor and ersatz-vernacular houses appeared around the edges of our cities. The style was so easy to copy that hundreds of builders seized on the fashion. It was so successful that it almost put architects out of a job. In the process, there was a betrayal of the original Arts and Crafts ideals. Instead of true frame structures there were false beams, there for decoration alone.

In continental Europe architects used different materials in a different way. In many countries experiments with a new, machine-made architecture were well under way in the first decade of the twentieth century and modern materials such as reinforced concrete and steel were being widely used. What is more, designers were beginning to put them to the service of a socialist architecture, in which these new materials and rapid, logical construction methods were used to create housing for all. Continental architects saw the morality of the Arts and Crafts Movement as a confirmation that their own, very different-looking, buildings were along the right lines. Modern materials could truly be displayed. And the most modern material of all was shining white concrete.

NEW LIFE, NEW HOUSES

The forms and patterns that architects created with concrete were abstract, simple and bold. Decoration, the set of devices that architects of the past had used to enliven

Concrete

Concrete is a mixture of cement, coarse aggregates (such as crushed stone), fine aggregates (such as sand) and water. When these ingredients are mixed the cement and water combine to make a binding material that holds the aggregates together. A concrete column, beam, floor plate, or other component is usually made by pouring the liquid concrete into a mould. This can be done at the building site or in a factory.

Concrete is strong under compression but very weak in tension. However, it can be reinforced. Steel rods or mesh are put into the mould and the concrete is poured around them. Further strength can be gained by prestressing concrete. There are different ways of doing this, but the idea is to use tensioned steel wires as the reinforcing material. In a floor panel, for example, the wires pull the concrete upwards to form a slightly arched shape that reduces sagging and cracking.

Reinforced concrete was invented in France in about 1852 and was used sporadically in building until the end of the nineteenth century. However, it did not make the impact on architects and engineers that iron had made earlier in the same century. It was only in the early twentieth century that they began to realize its immense potential. The French took the lead in using the material, notably architects such as Auguste Perret and engineers such as Eugéne Freysinnet (designer of the awesomely huge airship hangars at Orly).

British architects had experimented with concrete during the nineteenth century but took longer than the French to appreciate its potential. They used it in some high-quality houses, cinemas and other buildings of the 1930s, such as the de la Warr Pavilion, some of which are still among the best examples of the material's use in Britain.

the surfaces of their buildings, was swept away and they were left with simply the essence of walls, floors, and roofs. In Britain this abstract play of forms reached its ultimate in houses like High and Over, Buckinghamshire, designed by Amyas Connell. Built in 1929, it was one of the very first of its type in this country.

The building has a concrete frame. This is in fact infilled with brick, but the surfaces are covered with white render to give an all-over-concrete look. The unusual Y-shape plan catches the eye, which is led quickly to a concrete canopy that covers one area of the flat roof. The reason for this feature is that the house incorporates an open-air sleeping deck – suggesting an awareness on the part of the first owners of a movement promoting healthy living and embracing activities from callisthenics to sunbathing. This type of house, in other words, demanded of its occupants a rigorous way of life, far from the comforts to which most ordinary British people aspired. The masses were more likely to find what they wanted in a mock-Tudor house in the suburbs. Meanwhile, High and Over stands as aloof from the surrounding Amersham suburbs as its name suggests, confirming that the concrete style, intended at first to be available to all, became quickly the preserve of a few rich patrons.

▲ Houses by Amyas Connell, Amersham, Buckinghamshire.

THE MODERNIST STYLE

Concrete, though central to Modernism, was not its only feature. The Swiss architect and foremost Modernist, Le Corbusier, summarized five points which seemed to him to sum up the style. The first was the use of pillars or, as Le Corbusier called them, *pilotis*, to raise the building off the ground. In a house, for example, service areas like the garage or boiler room could be at ground level, amongst the *pilotis*, while the main rooms would be on the floors above. The second of Le Corbusier's five points was the provision of a roof garden, allowed by the flat roof. Third and fourth came freedom of interior plan and facades. These were

'A MODERN STATEMENT OF IDEALISM AND HOPE FOR THE FUTURE'

permitted by the use of a frame structure which meant that, with the weight of the building supported by columns, neither external nor internal walls had to be structural. Finally, Le Corbusier advocated strip windows to fill his interiors with light.

During the 1930s British architects began to adopt some of these ideas. An early, daring example of the style is the building designed by Joseph Emberton for the Royal Corinthian Yacht Club, Burnham-on-Crouch (1930–1). Here strip windows and flat roofs are highly functional – they offer spectators superb views of a long stretch of the river. A steel frame is used to support the structure but the base of the building is reinforced concrete.

But Le Corbusier's five points were aimed more specifically at domestic architecture. Houses like Maxwell Fry's Sun House, Hampstead (1935) take up the challenge. It is raised above its garage, is flat roofed, and has ribbons of windows on the main facade. These stylistic points were also to be found in blocks of flats by modernist architects; the influential London blocks Highpoint 1 and Highpoint 2, designed by Russian émigré Berthold Lubetkin and his radical practice, Tecton, in the 1930s are examples.

THE DE LA WARR PAVILION

Perhaps the best, most shining example of early Modernist architecture in Britain is a unique building, the de la Warr Pavilion at Bexhill-on-Sea, East Sussex (1935–6). It has a good claim to its relationship with the socialist architecture of Europe: the idea of the Labour Party mayor of Bexhill, Earl de la Warr, it was built as a multi-purpose leisure centre, containing a theatre, library, and cafés, that was made available to everyone. Its architects were German Jewish exile Erich Mendelsohn and Russian-born Serge Chermayeff. Mendelsohn had designed Modernist icons such as the Einstein Tower, Potsdam, a futuristic structure containing an observatory and laboratory, before fleeing the Nazis.

The Einstein Tower, white and modernistic, is a tall building. The de la Warr Pavilion is longer and lower. These qualities make it seem more British; indeed its long, low lines and the emphasis on horizontals that it displays seem related to the lines of the country houses designed by Lutyens and his peers. In other ways it could hardly be more different.

On one side of the pavilion is the blank, white wall of the theatre. The other side, by contrast, has broad windows and balconies from which those in the building's cafés can look out to sea. A glazed semicircular stair tower separates these two aspects and provides a focal point for the facades.

The stairway also dominates the interior. Modernism rejected ornament as a crime but, with the elegant turn of the staircase and the counterpoint between the upright glazing bars of the window and the curve of the handrail, no ornament is needed; the sculptural form of the building is enough to delight the eye. The eye is also delighted by the sea view. Mendelsohn and Chermayeff ensured that this was available all the year round by running hot water pipes up the window mullions to keep the glass clear, an engaging gesture towards the vagaries of the British climate.

The de la Warr Pavilion, then, looks like a Modernist version of the doctrine of truth to materials. Indentations in the wall surface seem to show how the concrete was constructed. In fact, it was not so simple. The recession of the 1930s meant that the builders had to go for the cheapest option: a structural steel frame supporting concrete outer cladding. The frame was welded together

▼ The main façade of the de la Warr Pavilion, Bexhill-on-Sea, by Erich Mendelsohn and Serge Chermayeff.

on site, a technique imported from Germany to save steel and used here for the first time in Britain. Cheating to save money did not make the building any less effective, however, and it still stands as an exemplar of its style.

PLASTIC FORMS

Concrete, with its potential for ease of construction, clean, white surfaces and curving, sculptural forms, caught on amongst the Modernist architects of Britain. The de la Warr Pavilion is just one example among a number of notable buildings of the 1930s that used concrete in this plastic, sculptural way. The most sculptural of all is hardly a building at all; it is the 1934 penguin pool at Regent's Park Zoo, London, designed by Lubetkin and Tecton. The pool is arranged around a pair of concrete ramps that spiral around each other with little in the way of visible support. They form a visual coup, as well as a delightful environment for the birds, and these twin qualities won Lubetkin fame as an architect who could fuse modern materials with user-friendly spaces.

Builders were soon using the sculptural qualities of concrete in housing for humans. Apartment blocks, until then not the most British of building types, became popular, and architects used concrete to create balconies that protruded from the walls with, like Lubetkin's penguin ramps, no obvious

▸ Penguin Pool, Regents Park Zoo, London, by Lubetkin and Tecton. Buckinghamshire.

support. In fact, they were using that most modern of structural devices, the cantilever, a principle that we now take for granted on structures as varied as stairways and railway bridges.

INDUSTRIAL MODERN

In Britain, where the climate discourages features like balconies and open-air sun decks, Modernism seemed more appropriate as a style for industrial buildings. So when John Boot, of Boots the Chemist, wanted to concentrate his factory and office facilities on a single site in Nottingham he did not commission an architect. The man he called on was Owen Williams, an engineer with a brilliant understanding of modern design. Prosaically known as the D10 building, this is Britain's first office and factory complex built primarily of concrete and glass. It is entirely true to these materials. The concrete columns are visible and their shape, mushrooming out below the floors, shows how they hold the structure up: form follows function.

'A TRIUMPH OF ENGINEERING OVER APPLIED STYLE'

Glass is used all over the outer surfaces of the building. Light filters down through the roof, which is made of concrete panels pierced with glass discs. There are 220,000 of these discs all told, and galleries and light wells pierce the floors in many places so that the light they admit can reach each of the building's four storeys. Light also floods in through a large central atrium. More glass replaces the walls, for there are no walls in the conventional sense, just two hectares of glazing supported on slender steel bars and interrupted only by the horizontal lines of the floors. It is not all clear. A combination of rough-cast and polished plate glass is used to let in plenty of light without too much glare.

D10 is vast – twice the length of a football pitch, 20 metres high and with 65,000 square metres of floor space. As well as being huge, it is hugely efficient, qualities that are summed up by the vast central atrium which allows materials to be transported easily up and down, as well as across, the building. The factory is built of industrial materials – steel, glass, and concrete. It is efficiently engineered. Yet it is also a pleasant building to work in, sunny and light. Some seventy years on, it is still used for its original purpose.

▸ Boots D10 Building, near Nottingham, by Owen Williams.

MODERN OR MODERNE?

As the 1930s went on, the features of modern architecture became more widely acceptable in Britain. Even if people did not want modern houses, they were happy with modern factories. And modern structures started to appear in other places. A more flamboyant style was also emerging that brought new kinds of architecture before the public eye. Ironically, it was a style of decoration, what is now known as Art Deco. This was the style of sharp lines, bold geometry and bright colours that became fashionable in Europe after an exhibition of decorative and industrial art in Paris in 1925. By the 1930s it was catching on in Britain, especially in showy buildings like cinemas and ones owned by high-profile organizations such as newspapers. Its ornate decoration was a marked contrast to all-white Modernism, yet at the same time Art Deco buildings displayed many of the features – flat roofs, strip windows, and white walls – that made modern buildings so distinctive. It was an odd hybrid and it produced eccentric results – from Odeon cinemas to Owen Williams's famous black-clad *Daily Express* building in London – which have always inspired affection.

It also inspired a more muted style, sometimes called Moderne, which combined the white walls and strip windows of Modernism with some of the colours and geometries of Art Deco. Many housing developments were built in this style, some with flat roofs, others with pitched roofs of green tiles, and these did something to bring a more modern aesthetic on to Britain's streets. So did Charles Holden, who designed a series of distinguished modern stations for the Piccadilly Line on London's underground. Flat-roofed, minimally decorated, well lit with generous windows and innovative light fittings, and set off by features like towers or high circular halls, they brought modern architecture closer to the people.

THE FESTIVAL OF BRITAIN AND THE SOUTH BANK

In 1951 the Festival of Britain was held to inject a mood of optimism into a nation suffering from postwar austerity. Rationing had continued. People felt that they had, in a famous phrase of the day, 'won the war, but lost the peace'. The festival was a national celebration, but its heart was on the South Bank of the Thames in London. Here a group of exciting new buildings were erected to celebrate British culture: the Dome of Discovery, the famous, upward-pointing Skylon, the Royal Festival Hall. Modern architecture was coming to the people once more.

Of all these structures only the Festival Hall, designed by the London County Council architects department, was meant to be permanent. Its style is a rather gentle form of Modernism achieved by bringing together elements of two movements from the past: the Modernist style itself and the Arts and Crafts sensibility. So glass and concrete are combined in the interior with warm, friendly materials like polished wood and brass to create a softened version of the modern style.

The Festival Hall's site presented the architects with a difficulty. All day and every evening, trains thunder their way across the South Bank towards Hungerford Bridge and Charing Cross station. Beneath the site runs the

▲ Royal Festival Hall, London, as it appeared soon after its opening in 1951.

Bakerloo Line, connecting Charing Cross with Waterloo. Sound insulation threatened to be a problem. The architects rose to this challenge by placing the auditorium in the middle of the building and wrapping it in insulating staircases, foyers, bars, restaurants, exhibition areas, and other gathering spaces.

As a result, the Festival Hall has more and better public spaces around it than most performance venues. The architects lavished great care on these areas. There is a beautiful sense of fluid space here, and plenty of room for people to move around the building with ease. Even today, fifty years after the building was opened, it provides a popular convivial meeting place in the heart of London.

From the outside, the glass northern facade of the hall reflects the sky. From within, the foyers offer views of the concrete walkways and neighbouring buildings, such as the Hayward Gallery and Queen Elizabeth Hall, erected during the 1960s. By this time, British architects had developed the relationship between concrete and craftsmanship still further. The gallery was made by building wooden moulds, known as shuttering, and pouring the concrete into place. By shot-blasting the wood before making the moulds, the builder could exaggerate the grain so that it leaves a clearly visible imprint on the concrete after setting. The effect is rather surreal but it offers, as it were, a lesson in how to build a concrete structure. Anyone can understand, straight away, that it must have been made using a wooden mould.

Giving concrete the imprint of wood should have softened the surface, contributing to that very British marriage of Modernism and Arts and Crafts. But it did not turn out like that. The concrete quickly weathered badly to a dirty grey and the style soon became labelled Brutalism, a uniquely British style that received widespread condemnation.

Today, many of the 1960s concrete walkways have been demolished in a scheme to upgrade the South Bank and make the public spaces outside as

'A STATEMENT OF BRITAIN'S NOT-SO-CONFIDENT NEW IDENTITY'

effective as those inside the Festival Hall. As this has been done, new vistas of the hall have appeared and we see it again as its architects intended it to be seen. It is a symbolic moment in the difficult British relationship with concrete.

THE RIGHT STYLE?

For much of the nineteenth century architects argued about which was the 'right' style in which to build. Followers of Pugin and Ruskin, especially, were convinced that Gothic was not only effective architecturally, but was actually morally superior to any other style. In the mid-twentieth century architects still wanted a style that was both effective and morally correct. This is one reason why they stuck so resolutely to Modernism. Modernism embraced truth to materials; it involved responding precisely to the demands of function (you built just enough space, no more, no less); and it seemed fitting for an industrial society. Modernism seemed right.

In the hands of a great architect with adequate funding, the modern style could deliver the goods. But the architect needed the time to work out the building from first principles, and the resources to provide it with all the services it needed. What happened in the 1950s and 1960s was that, faced with a demand for cheap, rapidly constructed buildings – especially housing – architects and clients used Modernism as a way of building quickly, using the resources of steel and concrete without the care over planning and details that made good Modernist buildings successful.

Concrete and steel technology was, anyway, the obvious way to go. It enabled the sort of prefabrication that allowed apartment blocks and houses to be built at rapid speed and low cost. It seemed just what was needed to rebuild Britain quickly after the war. At the same time, planners addressed the question of how to deal with the increasing population of motor cars. It appeared logical to separate the noisy, smelly vehicles from pedestrians, and flats and public buildings were built with elevated walkways in what seemed like a liberating, humanizing solution.

In fact, many of the buildings were dehumanizing. They lacked the facilities their residents needed and were frequently poorly built. The walkways were at best windswept and unpleasant, at worst the haunts of muggers and other criminals. A style that was meant to be popular ended up despised by the people it was supposed to serve.

What was the way out of this malaise? As architects began to realize in the 1970s, there were several. In other words, architecture had to leave behind the dogma that there was one true style which would do for any building in any situation. So a number of different styles emerged at the end of the twentieth century. They all involved rejection of the purist ethos of Modernism and a deeper consideration of how buildings would actually be used. Many of them also entailed a searching look at how we relate with the past, an issue that Modernism had left behind.

SCULPTING WITH CONCRETE

Not that architects left 'modern materials' behind. Some of the most successful late twentieth-century buildings are made of concrete. But they are more likely than the buildings of early Modernism to show off the curvaceous, plastic qualities that concrete can achieve. The Barbican Centre, a vast development of apartments in the City of London built around a school and arts centre, is a successful scheme that makes highly creative use of concrete. It was designed by architects Chamberlain, Powell and Bon in the 1960s and took some twenty-five years to complete. Many features of the buildings in the Barbican – the balconies, towers, and sections of the walls – are like celebrations of the sculptural qualities of poured concrete. So too are the curving barrel vaults in some of the upper flats – they are said to be a homage by one of the architects to the Roman buildings he admired. Indeed, the whole complex has something of the grandeur of a Roman forum, a grandeur tempered by the courtyards and water gardens at its heart, by the medieval church which the apartments surround and, appropriately, by the fragments of London's ancient Roman wall nearby.

The same firm's New Hall, a Cambridge college of the 1960s, makes similarly plastic use of concrete. The complex includes a white dome, the surface of which is cut away in segments rather like the dome of an observatory. Semi-domed turrets and a spacious library, barrel-vaulted like a Roman basilica, add to the monumental effect. As at the Barbican, the buildings are enhanced by the use of water in the garden.

Other architects created interesting shapes in concrete without allusions to past styles. Denys Lasdun, commissioned to design Britain's

Lifts

It had been possible to build tall buildings for centuries – the towers of the great medieval cathedrals show that clearly enough. But there was a problem if they were designed designed to accommodate people on their upper floors: access. Simple hoists, using ropes and pulleys to haul loads to the upper storeys of warehouses, were easy to construct. But when the load included people, there was a safety issue: what happened if the rope broke?

Famously, the solution was provided by the American inventor Elisha Graves Otis in 1852. The Otis Safety Elevator had a spring mechanism that engaged in a set of teeth which caught the lift car if the cable broke. Five years later, Otis's company was supplying passenger elevators to New York stores. The way was open for tall office and apartment buildings.

Modern lifts are powered by electric motors rather than the steam engines of Otis's first models, and can travel at up to about 510 metres a minute. Technology could enable them to go faster still, but discomfort sets in with rapid air-pressure changes at higher speeds and faster rates of acceleration.

National Theatre (completed 1975), again brought concrete to the South Bank. For the walls he used a mould-poured concrete similar to that used on the Hayward Gallery. But the effect is not quite so brutal and unforgiving. There are good reasons for this. One is that the building draws in the eye. Lasdun makes great interplay with vertical structures (such as the

▲ Flats at the Barbican, London, by Chamberlain, Powell and Bon.

▸ 1960s concrete construction on the South Bank, London.

theatre's fly towers) and horizontals (terraces that jut out to give views over the river and continue indoors to provide foyer and front-of-house areas). Another is that the foyers are generous spaces which allow people to circulate, eat, drink, and buy their tickets in relative comfort. There is also room enough for the entertainment to spill out of the auditoria into the foyers, so that people can enjoy short, early evening musical performances over a drink before catching the main event of the night. Last, but not least, the three auditoria themselves have proved successful performance spaces.

HIGH-TECH

An alternative route for architects was to stay ultramodern but look beyond concrete. Technology provides all sorts of new opportunities – new ways of building metal frames, new types of tougher, more versatile glass, new ways of stabilizing tall buildings in high winds, new ways of supporting curtain walls of glass, new materials, and so on. Displaying and celebrating this technology, High-tech buildings can look different from anything that has gone before.

One of the great rallying cries in the High-tech movement was provided by Richard Rogers and Renzo Piano's famous Pompidou Centre (1977) in

Paris. Here all the building services, from air-conditioning ducts to escalators, are hung on the outside to provide vast, open floors inside.

In the same year as the Pompidou Centre opened, Britain got its own High-tech building for the arts: Norman Foster's Sainsbury Centre for the Visual Arts at the University of East Anglia, Norwich. Clad in panels of white anodized aluminium and glass, the centre is much more restrained than its French contemporary. Yet its huge steel trusses, exposed at either end of the building, are still a celebration of engineering and a reminder that High-tech buildings like these owe more than a little to great Victorian engineers such as Isambard Kingdom Brunel.

Like the great Victorians, Foster and Rogers are painstaking about details, and the refinement of their buildings is what sets them apart. The fine finish and attention to everything down to the light fittings and door handles makes structures like Richard Rogers's Lloyd's Building (1986) literally shine. The pipes, stairways, and glass-sided lifts exposed on the outsides of the building gleam in the sun and glow with artificial light at night. Beautifully finished, the building looks expensive, and it is. But it is also a celebration of engineering and what it can achieve.

The modern materials used in High-tech structures can look different in other ways. During the 1980s the use of new fabrics, coated with protective substances such as Teflon, led to a number of buildings that look like vast tents. Michael Hopkins is a master of the tented roof, as his Schlumberger Research Laboratories (1985; see page 71) and Mound Stand at Lord's Cricket Ground (1987) have shown. But buildings like these are one-offs.

'RADICALLY NEW BUILDINGS HAVE ALMOST ALWAYS BEEN CONTROVERSIAL'

CITY LIVING

How has modern architecture affected the way people live? The success of the motor car has strengthened the tendency, which started at the opening of the twentieth century, to move towards the suburbs. Whereas in the early years of the century suburb-dwellers caught a train or tube to work, people now drive. In a car, an extra mile or two added on to the daily journey is hardly significant, so houses can be further and further apart. This has

▸ Norman Foster's
Sainsbury Centre for the
Visual Arts, Norwich.

strengthened the British desire to extend personal space beyond the walls of the house into the garden, increasing the sprawl of the suburbs still more.

New building types, from the petrol station to the superstore, have followed in the wake of out-of-town life. Most archetypal of all, the symbol of the decay of town centres, is the shopping mall. The Trafford Centre, some six miles from the centre of Manchester, is as good an example as any. Malls like this are clever exercises in packaging. They offer a bigger, brighter, more comprehensive 'shopping experience' in an enclosed, air-conditioned city where people can park and move around without worrying about the weather. There may be something technicolour and futuristic about the typical mall, but it is dressed in a whole wardrobe of architectural styles from the past. Columns might be Greek, Roman, or even Egyptian in inspiration; the arched glazed roof a tamed version of a Victorian train shed; the shopfronts any style at all. What is more, most of these stylistic effects are likely to be fake, plasterboard or plywood stage scenery that has little or nothing to do with the structure.

All this, of course, reflects the all-inclusive nature of the mall. The idea is that it is possible to buy anything here, and then eat food from anywhere in the world in a themed restaurant. But the architecture that contains

'GETTING MODERN-LOOKING BUILDINGS BUILT IN THE TWENTIETH CENTURY HAS BEEN A STRUGGLE'

this activity is too often a tame pastiche, lacking the stylistic mix that the Victorians managed.

Out-of-town areas need not be dull. Dickson Jones have produced a supermarket on the outskirts of Plymouth that almost looks as if it is about to sprout wings. The building, in most ways conventional, has been given a canopy made up of a series of sail-like shapes which look as if they are twisting as you pass. It provides a welcome contrast to the cool aluminium cladding of the facade, the whole giving a new look to a tired building type. Impressive as it is, though, it is still only a supermarket. It does not change people's lives any more than any other out-of-town store.

▲ Waterside, the British Airways Headquarters, by Nils Thorp.

What happens when a building really does try to change the way its out-of-town users lead their lives? A suburban office complex, like Nils Thorp's 1997 headquarters for British Airways at Waterside, near Heathrow, provides one answer. British Airways brought around 2,800 employees here from various city locations. Once in the complex employees hardly need to go out. They have their own banks, shops, cafes, restaurants, hairdressers, newsagents, and even fitness centres, connected by a central atrium that works like a private high street. They work in six connected open-plan office blocks. Intelligent mobile phones and laptop computers provide great flexibility – people can work anywhere in the building, and need not be tied down to one personal office space. Less a building than a total environment, the complex smacks of great freedom, but leaves one longing for the real freedom of the true city.

REGENERATING THE CITIES

Shopping malls are criticized for killing town centres. Why should people put up with the hassle of town-centre shopping when they can have everything they need under one roof? In some places, though, the city centre is fighting back. Manchester's Northern Quarter, a once thriving district which suffered a twentieth-century decline, is a case in point. Urban regeneration, together with an influx of young musicians, designers, and architects, have given the area a bold new identity. It is still rather run down, but it works, and it provides people with a mix of buildings that offer places to live, work, eat, shop and be entertained without leaving the area.

Many of the Northern Quarter's structures are conversions and upgradings. Ours is not the first generation to convert old buildings for different uses. But the combined influences of the green movement, conservation issues, and the speed with which buildings become outmoded has meant that conversion is now a major aspect of the building industry. In Manchester, architects Stephenson Bell have led the way. Their warehouse conversion offers flats opening on to a bright central atrium where old and new features come together. A Victorian roof framed in wrought iron is offset against new galvanized-steel mesh; modern doors and fittings counterpoint old brickwork. The building's juxtaposition of old and new gives it a knowing, urban quality, something which is seen in the same firm's Quay Bar, another highlight of the Northern Quarter.

More strikingly new is Whitby and Bird's bridge, a white sweeping curve. This structure displays a more dynamic contrast with the old features – the infrastructure of canals and railway bridges from Manchester's industrial past – which surround it. In the evening the bridge is busy with nightlife as people walk to and from the area's bars and clubs. Bars like Mash and Air, decorated in strident orange and lime green, might look at first glance like refugees from the 1960s given a new lick of bright paint. Yet the regeneration goes more than skin-deep. Portholes behind the bar look on to the stainless steel cylinders of a micro-brewery. The beer you drink is actually brewed in the bar, a potent example of how functions – manufacturing, retail, entertainment – come together in a living city. It is symbolic, too, that this is a *micro*-brewery. The Northern Quarter is not a townscape of vast buildings and big civic statements. It works on a small, local scale, with small shops and businesses supplying local needs, with local designers having an input into how their district looks, and with local residents both earning and spending their money here to create a growing local economy.

THE POSTMODERN CITY

In the 1980s the redeveloped Docklands seemed to offer hope for working life in London with flagship office space that would enable companies to expand eastwards from the old and crowded City. Its central, towering symbol was Canary Wharf, with its office tower designed by Cesar Pelli and its surrounding collection of lower-rise office buildings, shops, and leisure facilities. Londoners watched in fascination as the country's tallest structure quickly rose to its 250-metre height and as the varied, mostly Postmodern, buildings around it took shape. But then came the crunch. Olympia and York, the ambitious firm of Canadian developers behind the scheme, hit financial trouble, Britain's 1980s property boom came to an end and, when Canary Wharf opened its doors in 1991, the complex suddenly seemed less glamorous.

Canary Wharf is certainly grand. The awesome entrance area of the tower, with its banks of lifts whisking workers to their offices in the sky, is like a temple. But when they get to their offices, many find that they are located too near the centre of the building to benefit from the magnificent views. In any case, Canary Wharf's grandeur is of an alien, imported kind, like a piece of corporate Chicago or New York towed in and moored by the Thames – one of its buildings was even dubbed the Brownstone, in honour of the New York houses that inspired it. This alien style, and the oddly detached position of Docklands from

▾ No. 1 Poultry, the post-modern complex at the heart of the City of London, designed by James Stirling and Michael Wilford.

'AS IF THE ECLECTIC MIX OF STYLES HAS BEEN DRAWN OUT OF THE CITY THAT SURROUNDS IT'

the City proper, have kept Canary Wharf apart, making it more like a suburb than part of a city.

James Stirling and Michael Wilford, architects of the office, shopping, and restaurant building at No. 1 Poultry, show that the British can build effective Postmodern buildings in the heart of a city. No. 1 is near the centre of London's financial district and is directly above a tube entrance – from the light well its occupants can watch passengers coming and going. Its phantasmagoria of styles is drawn from the city that surrounds it.

The building has often been compared to a great ship sailing towards its neighbours, the Bank of England and the Mansion House, pillars of the London establishment. Ship-like it certainly is, with its pointed front end and clock tower that resembles a funnel. In addition it draws on a variety of architectural and artistic styles, from the Renaissance (the garden on the roof) to Art Deco, combining them with Postmodern hallmarks such as polychrome striped masonry and seasoning them with a virtuoso play of shapes and forms – cylinders and cuboids, segmental arches and flat-topped openings, pointed bays and recessed windows. Truth to materials hardly matters here; no one cares whether or not the gorgeous stonework of the exterior walls holds the building up. The important thing is that it looks good.

A Postmodern building can look good in any way its designer chooses. Gone is the straitjacket of Modernism that dictated that all buildings should be flat-roofed and white. In contrast, Postmodernism says you can have anything you want – glazed tiles on the wall, primary-coloured window frames, wooden deck-like cladding on the ceilings. You can also make raids on historical styles, adding features such as columns and pediments, and details from any style from Egyptian to Renaissance. You can be witty, juxtaposing the styles in bizarre ways. Even architects who do not want to build in an out-and-out Postmodern style have been freed by the movement. At the beginning of the twenty-first century the possibilities seem endless.

OLD CLIENTS, NEW BUILDINGS

Again and again in this exploration of shocking buildings, we have seen how the establishment – the invading Romans, the medieval church, the eighteenth-century aristocracy, our Victorian rulers – have commissioned buildings in the forefront of design, structures that amazed their contemporaries and revised people's expectations about what buildings should be like. It should not be surprising, then, that at the turn of the twenty-first century some of the most remarkable, up-to-date buildings are to be found in the holy of holies of the Establishment, the last bastion of traditionalism – the headquarters of Britain's 'summer game', Lord's Cricket Ground.

The MCC's affair with new, radical architecture began with the Mound Stand (1987) designed by Michael Hopkins, the architect of the Schlumberger Research Laboratories in Cambridge (see page 71). At Lord's, as at the laboratories, white tented roofs held up by masts and wires again dominate the scene. At Lord's they have a celebratory feel, suggesting a modern-day Festival of Britain – as well as the very real advantage of giving a free, uninterrupted view of the field of play. Hopkins has also made sure that spectators on the lower levels get a good view. Much of the stand's weight rests on a brick arcade at the back, and only a handful of columns interrupt the expanse of seating at the lower, arena level. The large stand seems to hover with very little visible support.

▲ The Mound Stand at Lord's, designed by Michael Hopkins.

The authorities at Lord's followed their commission of Michael Hopkins with another stand by a prominent contemporary architect: Nicholas Grimshaw. But most revolutionary of all the recent structures at the cricket ground is the new Media Centre (1999), designed by Future Systems, a firm that specializes in using materials and techniques more familiar in mass-production industries like motor manufacture. The centre looks unlike any other building and for good reason: it was built in a unique way. It is made entirely of aluminium, a material that is light, very malleable and, unlike steel, does not rust. The metal is coated in resin to give it a smooth, high-gloss finish.

The aluminium has been made into a semi-monocoque structure. In other words, the metal outer skin of the building, which is welded to ribs and other stiffeners, actually forms part of the structure, a technique that is more familiar to car designers and boat builders than architects. So, appropriately, the Media Centre was not built in a conventional way. The structure's individual

'LOOKS DOWN ON THE GROUND LIKE THE LENS OF A GIANT CAMERA'

components were made by a firm of boat builders in Cornwall who used computerized lasers to precision-cut the metal to size and then welded the sections together to produce larger components. These were then taken by road to Lord's and assembled on site to make the finished building.

The result is a structure with a unique rounded shape which is both functional and beautiful. The curving themes are continued inside with soft, colourful doorways, windows, and stairs. The building had to look good on screen, since its image is broadcast all over the world whenever Lord's hosts an international cricket match, and the architects took some of their inspiration from television. They have compared its appearance to that of a large camera, its lens scrutinizing the field of play. They also drew inspiration for the building's curving lines from the sweeping oval of the ground itself. The centre's shape and size were also driven by the needs of its users. It is designed to accommodate with ease the reporters from television, radio, and the press who cover international cricket; and it is tall to give them the best possible view. It is a view, and a building, that its early users show every sign of enjoying.

▾ Lord's Media Centre: the interior.

Buildings like the Media Centre and No 1 Poultry give hope for architecture at the beginning of the twenty-first century. Their engagement with both past traditions and present users, their vibrant use of form and colour, their care with materials and finishes, their daring to be different in the most conservative of contexts – all these are attributes of their quality. They are shared in buildings by many other architects working at the turn of the century, from High-tech masters such as Richard Rogers and Norman Foster to virtuosi of form and colour like Michael Hopkins and John Outram. They are qualities, too, which are shared with the best of British buildings of the past, buildings which once shocked, and still inspire.

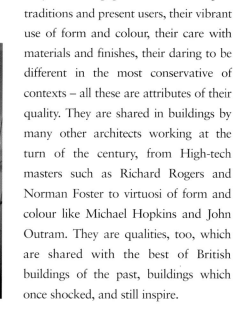

index

*Page numbers in italics
refer to the illustrations.*

A
aisled halls 81–2, 87
Albert Dock 137–9
Albert Hall 145, *146*
Albert Memorial 144, 145,
  145
aluminium 189
aqueducts 37
architectural styles and
  fashions 10–11
Art Deco 176–7
Arts and Crafts Movement
  166–7, 168, 169, 170,
  177, *166, 168*

B
Banqueting House 104–7,
  105, 106
Barbican Centre 180,
  181, *181*
barns 79, 81, *80, 81*
Baroque style 107
Bath 27–9, 122–4, *27, 28,
  122, 123*
bathhouses 27, 28–9,
  34–6, 38, *28*
Bayleaf 82, *82*
Bedford Square, London
  120
Bignor Roman Villa 23–6,
  24, 25, 26
black-and-white houses
  91–4, *86, 93*
bricks 10, 23, 83, 112,
  168–9, *113*
British Airways head-
  quarters 185, *185*
British Museum 126–7
Brutalism 178–9, *182*
Burrell Collection 161–2
Butser Ancient Farm
  13–14, *14*

C
Caerphilly Castle 89
Canary Wharf 70, 161,
  187
Canterbury cathedral 57–8

castles, Norman 45
cathedrals and churches
  10–11, 22, 42–6, 48–54,
  55, 56, 57–71
Channel Four Building
  100–1, *101*
chimneys 83–4, 86
Chiswick House 108–10,
  108
The Circle 131, *131*
classical style 38, 102,
  107, 123, 130, 145, 147,
  150–1
concrete 35, 41, 165, 170,
  171, 174–5, 178, 180–1
Coventry Cathedral 42–3,
  68–9, *43, 69*
cruck construction 77–80,
  80
Crystal Palace 156–60,
  157, 159
CZWG 100, 101, 131,
  100, 131

D
D10 (Boots building)
  175–6, *176*
de la Warr Pavilion 165,
  172–4, *165, 173*
Deanery Gardens 167–9,
  168
Decorated style 60–1,
  62–4, 143, *62, 63*
Docklands 187–8
Doncaster Dome 38
Durham cathedral 51–4,
  55, 56, *51, 52, 53, 54, 55*

E
Early English Gothic
  58–60
Edinburgh 124–5, 126,
  124, 126
Ely cathedral 48, 62–4,
  62, 63

F
farmhouses and manor
  houses 82–4, 86
fireproofing 138
Fishbourne 21

flying buttresses 56, 58
forts, Roman 16, 18, 31,
  34, 36, *19*
frame and truss
  construction method 77

G
Georgian style 115–21,
  128
Glass Building 100, 101,
  100
glass and glazing 10, 33,
  65, 69, 70–1, 84, 92,
  119, 156–60, 161–3,
  175, *65*
glasshouses 154–6, 160
Globe Theatre 99
Gloucester Cathedral
  10–11, 50, 64, 66–7, *67*
Gothic Revival 11, 142–4,
  147, 148
Gothic style 10, 57–64,
  66–7, 68, 145, 179
Gothick 115, 143
Great Coxwell barn 81, *81*
Greek revival 126–8

H
Hadrian's Wall 29–32, *13,
  30, 31*
half-timbered buildings 8, 9
Hampstead Garden
  Suburb 166–7, *166*
Hardwick Hall 94–7, *95,
  97*
Hawksmoor, Nicholas 107
High and Over 171
High-tech 100–1, 182–3
Holkham Hall 102, 103,
  111, 113–14, *103, 114*
Houses of Parliament
  146–7
Housesteads 36–7

I
Imax cinema, London
  70–1, *70*
Iron Age houses 13–14,
  33, *14*
iron-framed buildings
  152–4, *151, 153, 154*

J
jetties 77
Jones, Inigo 102, 104,
  105, 106, 107, 109, 117
Judge Institute of
  Management Studies
  38, 39, 40

K
Kent, William 110, 111
Kew Gardens 115, 154–6,
  154, 156

L
Lasdun, Denys 130–1,
  130
latrines, Roman 36–7
Leicester University
  Engineering Building
  161–2
Leigh Court 79, 80, *80*
lifts 136, 181
Lincoln cathedral 59, 63
Little Moreton Hall 91–4,
  93
Liverpool 68, 137–9,
  150–1, 153, *150*
Lloyd's Building 183
Lord's Cricket Ground
  183, 189–90, *189, 190*
Lutyens, Sir Edwin 167–9,
  168

M
Manchester 147–50,
  185–7, *148, 149, 186*
marble 21
medieval and Tudor
  buildings 8, 10–11, 42–67,
  72–98
Mereworth Castle 108
Midland Grand Hotel 132,
  133, 140, 141, 142, *133,
  141, 142*
mock-Tudor 98–9, 169,
  98
Moderne 177
Modernism 130, 171–7,
  179, 180
mosaics 10, 24–6, *26*

N
Nash, John 127–9
National Glass Centre 163, *163*
New Hall, Cambridge 180
New House, Wadhurst 40
Newington Green 87
No. 1 Poultry 187, 188, *187*
Norman buildings 45–56
Norwich cathedral 48

O
Olivier Theatre, Bedales School 99–100, *99*
Oriel Chambers 153, *153*
Outram, John 39–40, *38, 39, 40*

P
Palladian style 104, 108–11, 115
pantiles 23
pattern books 9, 117, *127*
Peckover House 116, *116*
Pendean 84
Penshurst Place 72–4, *73*
Perpendicular style 59, 64, 66, 69, 84
Peterborough cathedral 48, 49, 50, *49*
Piece Hall 38
Postmodernism 10, 187–8
prefabrication 179
prodigy houses 94–7, *95, 97*
Pugin, A.W.N. 143, 146–7
Purbeck marble 47, 58

Q
quarrying 47, *47*

R
railway stations 9, 139–42, 160, 161, 162, *140, 162*
railway, underground 134–7, 177, *135, 136, 161*
Regent's Park 127–9, 174, *129, 174*
Richborough 17–18, *17*
Richmond Riverside 130
Ripon cathedral 59
roads, Roman 15, 16, 17, *15*
Rochester cathedral 55
Roman buildings 8, 9, 12–37

Romanesque style 46, 48, 51, 52, 56
Royal College of Physicians 130–1, *130*
Royal Corinthian Yacht Club 172
Royal Festival Hall 177–9, *178*
Rufford Old Hall 90–1

S
Sainsbury Centre for the Visual Arts 183, 184, *184*
St Albans 20–3, 46, *22*
St George's Hall, Liverpool 150–1, *150*
St John's church, Escomb 44, 45, *44*
St Pancras church 127
St Pancras station 9, 139–42, *140*
Salisbury cathedral 59
sash windows 119
Saxon churches 44–5, *44*
scaffolding 50
Schlumberger Research Laboratories 71, 183, *71*
shopping malls and leisure centres 38–9, 184–5
South Bank 177–9, 181–2, *182*
South Shields 33–4, *34*
Stanton Harcourt 89
Stephenson Bell 186, *186*
Stokesay Castle *91*
stone 47, 48, 50, 89
stucco 121, 124
suburbs 165–7, 169–70, 183–4

T
temples, Roman 27–8
terrazzo floors 23
thatching 85, *85*
timber-framed buildings 75–7, 87, 98, 99, 100
town houses 77, 86–7, 115–19, 120–1, *116*
towns, Roman 18–23
tracery and carving 59, 60, 61, 63, 64
twentieth-century architecture 164–90

U
underfloor heating, Roman 34–5, *34*
urban regeneration 185–7

V
vaults 35, 52–4, 56, 57, 61, 62, 66–7
Victoria and Albert Museum 6
Victorian buildings 9, 10, 11, 132–60
villas, Roman 23–6

W
water engineering 37
Watling Estate 169
wattle and daub 13, 75, 78, 83, *78*

Weald and Downland Museum 82–3, 85, 86, *78, 82, 85*
Wells cathedral 59–61, *60, 61*
Westminster Hall 87–9
Winchester cathedral 48
Wren, Christopher 107, 120
wrought iron and cast iron 152, 155, 158

Y
York cathedral 59

Picture Credits